Richard Rowett. (Courtesy of the Illinois State Historical Library)

RICHARD ROWETT

Thoroughbreds, Beagles, and the Civil War

by
Tom Emery

HISTORY IN PRINT
337 E. Second South St.
Carlinville, IL 62626

Library of Congress
Catalog Card No. 97-77565

ISBN 0-9661637-0-2

HISTORY IN PRINT
337 East Second South
Carlinville, IL 62626

Cover sketch taken from
Portrait and Biographical Record of Macoupin County, Illinois
(Chicago: Biographical Publishing Co., 1891).

Printed in United States of America

PINE HILL PRESS, INC.
Freeman, S. Dak. 57029

Contents

Acknowledgements

Just before I sat down to write what you are about to read, I was browsing through the acknowledgements of another book, in which were written the following words: "No book is ever written alone."

I know the feeling. There are countless individuals who provided invaluable assistance in the creation of this volume. From my initial research in the summer of 1990 to these last words of the project, they've been there throughout and will forever be appreciated.

First, I must thank Randy Studer of Vancouver, Wash., who, along with Rowett family descendants Ellen Klineline and her daughter, Judy Klineline, also of Vancouver, was a neverending source of help and information whenever I needed it. From his numerous phone calls, letters, and photocopies, Randy supplied me with a good portion of the intricate detail that I was able to implement into this book. One of the best parts of doing this book was meeting all sorts of people, and having the opportunity to meet all three of these individuals was most memorable.

In addition, this book would not have reached its final levels without the unending assistance of the staff and students of Lumpkin Library, Blackburn College, Carlinville, Illinois, including Lydia Forbes, Carol Schaefer, Mary DeMoss, Lynn Armstrong, Wayne Shipley, and the many others who gave me unlimited access to interlibrary loan books and any library facilities that I needed. What they do too often goes unnoticed, but I will always remember them, for their help can be traced to a large portion of the material in this volume.

Another member of the Blackburn staff that is due great thanks is Chuck Sutphen, Director of Academic Computing, for his generous use of the College computer facilities. The text that you read is a by-product of the equipment and know-how of the lab personnel, and I am indeed grateful.

Others that I am indebted to include the Carlinville Public

Library; the Illinois State Historical Library; the Illinois State Archives; the Indiana Historical Society Library; the Indiana State Library; the Multnomah County Library (Portland, Ore.); the Cairo (Ill.) Public Library; the Johnson County (Ind.) Public Library; Lincoln Library, Springfield, Ill.; Fort Donelson National Battlefield, Dover, Tenn.; Columbus-Belmont State Park, Ky.; Camp Butler National Cemetery, Springfield, Ill.; United States Army Military History Institute, Carlisle Barracks, Pa.;

Doris Jean Waren, Keeneland Library, Lexington, Ky.; Devon Goddard, Atlanta Historical Society; Phil Germann, Historical Society of Quincy and Adams County (Ill.); Joseph Wiley, National Beagle Club, Bedminster, N.J.;

Stacy Allen, Shiloh National Military Park historian; Theresa Fitzgerald, librarian, *Blood-Horse Magazine*, Lexington, Ky; Margaret Greene Rogers, executive director, Northeast Mississippi Museum Association, Corinth, Miss.; William R. Scaife, Cartersville, Ga.; Susan R. Nardinger, Great Falls, Mt.; Tom Herring, Benkelman, Neb.; Psyche Williams, Joliet, Ill.; Joan McKay, Payson, Ill.; Patty Lankford, *Thoroughbred Times,* Lexington, Ky.; Patricia Tomczak, Quincy University library;

Darrin and Barb Daugherty, Daugherty Photography, Carlinville, Ill; the staff of the Circuit Clerk, County Clerk, Recorder of Deeds, and Probate offices, Macoupin County Courthouse, Carlinville, Ill.;

Dale Sprague, Carlinville, Ill.; Rick Davis, WSMI Radio, Carlinville, Ill.; Denny Clanton, computer lab assistant, Blackburn College, Carlinville, Ill.; Dr. Jan Zimmerman, History Department Chair, Blackburn College, Carlinville, Ill.; Dr. Ren Draya, Instructor of English, Blackburn College, Carlinville, Ill.

And I'm sure that I've forgotten someone. When you have as many people to thank as I do, you always know that you're leaving someone important out. Let me say now that there are many others--who answered my letters in libraries across the nation, who referred me to people that could help, and who spent time looking up information on the most obscure subjects that I could throw at them--who deserve credit as well. Your efforts are appreciated.

Of all the people I must thank, though, I owe the most to my mother, Janice Emery, whose continued love and support is behind all of my accomplishments.

Tom Emery
August 1997

I
Beyond Cornwall

Richard Rowett was born on November 17, 1830 in East Looe, Cornwall, England, and that is where his story begins. If one should divide Rowett's life into two halves, one for the first part of his life and one for the second, then there is much more to tell in the second half. Little is known of the first years of Rowett's life as he grew to adulthood across the ocean.

London and the powerful British empire no doubt seemed far away to East Looe, a small village in far southwestern England on the southern shore of the county of Cornwall. Fair temperatures, the warmest in the country, and rolling terrain dominated this land, just a few miles from the famed offshore lighthouse at Eddystone.

The empire was engaged in another war with their former colonies of the United States of America when William Rowett married the former Jenny Williams on April 11, 1814 in East Looe. They soon started a large family of five boys and five girls. Their eighth child, Richard, was born in 1830 and christened in the Anglican parish of Saint Martin on Looe Bay on March 24, 1831.

The Rowett name (pronounced ROU-ett) was common in Cornwall and its villages, but it was of modest means. Richard was educated in a common school and learned the trade of a carriage trimmer, but he soon realized that he wanted more from life than just being a worker with his hands.

The young man studied history, oratory, and biographies, and his character grew strong with age. He soon wondered about far-away lands, lands that many of his countrymen were leaving their homes for, and what opportunities they offered to a bright young fellow who had grown into a well-informed, educated man.

Members of his own family wondered the same. In the early 1850s, two of the Rowett brothers and a sister left for Australia, and soon Richard was planning his own emigration--to the United States. By the spring of 1851, his decision was final, and in June he boarded a ship in Liverpool and sailed for a new life.

The ship docked in New York harbor on July 26, and Richard stepped into a new nation that was barely 75 years independent. Immigrants from Germany, Ireland, England, and Russia were pouring by the thousands into America, where the land was abundant and the opportunities seemingly endless. The westward movement had begun as great metropolises burgeoned across the East Coast and along major waterways. Hostilities over slavery were flaring as the possibility of civil war seemed closer, but there was much promise in this ever-expanding nation to anyone willing to work for it.

Richard settled in Johnson County in central Indiana, where many of the county's 12,101 residents were occupied in agriculture. It, too, was a bustling area centered around Franklin, the largest town in the county which offered merchant houses, men of trade and profession, and even an institution of learning, Franklin College.

Rowett spent three years in Johnson County, working for an establishment dealing in buggies, harnesses, and trimming. On October 9, 1854, he was naturalized as a citizen of the United States, pledging his loyalty to his new home and country.

But Indiana would not be his home for much longer. Nearing 24 years of age, Rowett again set out for new opportunities, moving westward and settling in central Illinois in a town called Carlinville.

II
Carlinville

When Rowett arrived in Carlinville in 1854, the town, the seat of Macoupin County, was barely a quarter of a century old. First settled in 1829 by Ezekiel Good, early settlers told of the surprising amount of water scattered across this "frog-pond kingdom." Macoupin Creek, for which the county was named, bisected the prairie lands, while the Carlinville River ran through the middle of the town.

A population count in 1853 totalled 790 residents in this rural community, but the number of physicians, such as Dr. John Logan, and lawyers, like John M. Palmer, were increasing. Palmer was arguably the leading citizen of the town, a county judge, state senator, and delegate to the Illinois constitutional convention of 1848. He would later enjoy one of the greatest political careers in Illinois history, serving as governor and U.S. Senator despite an idealist, impulsive nature that led him to change political parties five times (hence the name of his 1941 biography, *A Conscientious Turncoat*). Culture was also becoming evident in Carlinville; Blackburn Seminary (later known as Blackburn College) was founded in 1837 and began offering classes in 1858.

Carlinville, situated 45 miles south (a two-day journey on horseback at the time) from the state capital of Springfield, was a farming town, and Rowett soon found himself employed in the agricultural trade. He was also variously employed as a clerk and a carriage trimmer. In 1857, he was joined in Carlinville by his brother Joseph, who had come to America the previous year.

The youngest of the ten Rowett children, the 23-year-old Joe* had always been devoted to his brother, and they would remain lifelong companions. Like Richard, Joe worked various jobs, but they one day hoped to own their own cattle stock farm, complete with Jersey cattle, and, if they could come by them, thoroughbred horses.

The affable Richard quickly made friends in Carlinville.

According to Mary Hunter Austin, a local native who later achieved some national measure of fame as an author, Rowett and her father, George Hunter, struck up a friendship and became active in the town social scene. Austin says that the two men spent a great deal of time with each other, discussing the philosophies of Robert Ingersoll and the controversial new theory of evolution while attending church together or "rising to make a few remarks" whenever appropriate.

Well-mannered and conversational, "Dick" Rowett was a dark, bearded man of medium height and solid build who was carefully attired. A forceful speaker with a sense of wit, he soon became well-known to all in his new home.

His social life, though, did not include vices. He was a firm believer in temperance, never indulging in the social glass when others around him did. Rowett remained true to his temperance ideals throughout his life and was later commended as being ahead of his time on the issue.

Although he had lived in America for only a few years, Rowett developed a love and loyalty of his adopted country that rivaled the most patriotic of men. His emotions ran deep, as did those of everyone else; the 1850s were a time of strife and division as the United States was torn over slavery and states' rights.

Even in Macoupin County, those loyal to the Union cause were not in overwhelming number. Southern sympathies were clearly evident in a highly Democratic district that voted against Abraham Lincoln for President in both 1860 and 1864 and cast their ballots against local son Palmer for Republican governor in 1868. The two Carlinville newspapers, the *Free Democrat* (owned by Palmer and, not true to its name, a Republican outlet) and the *Spectator* traded barbs on every political issue, but were especially intense when it came to the Democratic support that prevailed in the county.

Dick Rowett would have none of this. He remained staunchly pro-Union with an opposition to slavery that had developed even before he became an American citizen. Austin claims that Rowett played a local role in the Underground Railroad that helped escaped slaves to freedom and also says that he was a frequent guest of a rural Palmyra family known for hiding runaway slaves.

Emotions continued to flare as the 1860 election neared, and with Lincoln's subsequent victory, the Southern cause took shape as states seceded one by one to form the fledging Confederate States of America. A war to preserve the Union was imminent, and it became a dark reality when Fort Sumter was fired upon the following April 12.

Tempers heated across the divided nation, and Carlinville was certainly no exception. The strong pro-Southern sentiment festered, much to Rowett's chagrin. He added to the tension of April 1861 by reportedly thrashing a county official who was a Southern sympathizer, an extreme act that reflected not only Rowett's own temper but also the high-strung emotional state that was prevalent in both North and South.

Lincoln called for 75,000 volunteers to put down the rebellion, and many times that number offered their services. It was later said that Rowett's voice was the first to be heard in Carlinville in defense of the Union, and within twenty-four hours of the call for troops, he volunteered to serve his adopted country of less than a decade. He helped raise a company of local men, including Joseph, and was himself named captain of the unit, christened the "Carlinville Invincibles."

After a grand sendoff from Carlinville, the Invincibles were mustered into service at Springfield on April 25 and became Company K of the Seventh Illinois Volunteer Infantry. Regiments were numbered on the basis of their date of muster, with the exemptions of the First through Sixth designations in deference to those units' service in the Mexican War. Many troops argued for the distinction of being the first to answer the call for volunteers, but the honor was accorded to the Seventh Illinois.

Following its muster, the Seventh was sent to Alton for training and was housed in the old state penitentiary. To the men, many of whom thought glory and adventure lay waiting, the poor quarters and harsh treatment at the old prison were a sharp awakening to what war really was. And its end would not come soon.

---

*There is uncertainty as to Joseph's date of birth, given in varying sources as 1833, 1834, and 1836, which is the date inscribed on his tombstone.

III
Campaigns in Tennessee

It soon became apparent that the original request for ninety days' service would not be enough to quelch the rebellion, a point further evidenced by the Union rout at Bull Run July 21. The call was then made for three years' service, and the Seventh was reorganized and mustered on July 25 for what looked to be a prolonged struggle.

The regiment was camped in southeastern Missouri through the late summer and early fall of 1861 and spent much of September pursuing rebels under Jeff Thompson, the notorious "Swamp Fox." Following that unsuccessful expedition, Rowett (since promoted to major) and the Seventh went into winter quarters at Fort Holt, Ky. on October 5. They had served over five months and, like most units, had done little; Northern troops were finding out that war was not all glory and adventure.

But an offensive was brewing. The brigade that included the Seventh was part of the District of Cairo, commanded by a relatively unknown brigadier general named Ulysses S. Grant. Grant planned to move against the Confederate river stronghold of Columbus, Ky. by threatening Belmont, Mo., just across the Mississippi. Occupation of Belmont meant that the North could cut off communications between Columbus and the Confederates in Missouri as well as helping to retain Kentucky, a border state, as Union territory.

As part of this attack, the Seventh's brigade (under Colonel John Cook) was sent southward from Fort Holt to Elliott's Mills to demonstrate against Columbus while Grant's main forces moved on Belmont on the Missouri side. Grant was repulsed in a largely indecisive battle, and the Seventh was ordered back to Fort Holt, where they spent most of the winter.

A smaller expedition to Columbus in January also did not capture that place in the only action the Seventh would see in the winter of 1861-62. They remained at Fort Holt until February 3, when they were ordered to Tennessee to join Grant's offensive against Forts Henry and Donelson.

By taking the forts, the Union would open routes of invasion along the Tennessee and Cumberland rivers while forcing the Confederates from Kentucky. Fort Henry, on the Tennessee River, was the weaker of the two positions and fell in a naval assault on February 6. The Seventh was stationed at the rear of the fort awaiting deployment, but the gunboats were all that was needed to secure the fort.

Still, the Seventh had not seen battle conditions, which was the case with most of the army. The Federals arrived at Fort Donelson, situated on the Cumberland River near Dover, Tenn., on February 12, and Cook's brigade was set up on the left flank, opposite the forces of Simon Bolivar Buckner in front of the fort.

Grant had effectively surrounded the rebels, and the attack began on February 13 as temperatures dropped from mild in the afternoon to nearly ten degrees that night. In their first real combat of the war, Rowett and the Seventh performed well, overcoming whatever nerves they may have felt. They remained on the left throughout the three-day offensive and were part of the last charge on Fort Donelson on February 15 by the Second Division under Brigadier General Charles F. Smith. Cook's brigade advanced on the eastern part of Buckner's lines while another of Smith's brigades moved on the Union's extreme left, and this charge tightened the vice on the Confederates. The men of the Seventh were among the first to scale the walls of Fort Donelson, preceded only by the 14th Iowa.

Buckner, left holding the bag as his superiors passed command and escaped, accepted Grant's famous "unconditional surrender" terms on February 16, and the fort and 14,623 troops fell to the Union. Smith and his charge were credited by Grant as the reason for the Federal victory, and Smith was promoted to major general. The Union suffered 2,832 casualties, and the Seventh incurred its share, mainly from Rowett's old Company K.

Rowett was praised for his actions at Donelson in the

9

first of numerous compliments found in the *History of the Seventh Illinois Volunteer Infantry*, a firsthand account by Daniel Leib Ambrose, who served in Company H. At Donelson, Ambrose stated that Rowett "deserved the plaudits of all" and was "found where all the brave were found." "Enthusiastic, but not rash" were Rowett's actions and, said Ambrose, "none but could admire his dash." While Ambrose's words throughout the book are heavily overstated and often flowery, they nonetheless give the reader a good idea of Rowett's ability in battle.

More than anything else, Rowett was relieved that he stood up and faced the danger at Fort Donelson. "I never felt so happy in all my life, " said Rowett in Ambrose, " as when before that rebel battery that first day; happy because I there discovered that I had a heart to face the cannon's mouth, which I did not feel certain of having until then."

****

On February 20 the Seventh's commander, Lieutenant Colonel A.J. Babcock, took leave due to illness, and the reins of the regiment were given to Rowett. After being ordered to Nashville, the brigade was loaded onto steamers, and the Seventh, aboard the *Fairchild,* sailed southward for Pittsburg Landing, near Savannah, Tenn.

Just getting there was an arduous journey as some regiments spent over a week on board waiting to disembark. By March 18, the Seventh had sat on the *Fairchild* for eleven days and was extremely anxious to get off the boat. Forced to drink polluted water from the Tennessee, many of the men became ill. After 13 days of misery on the steamer, the Seventh was finally ordered to disembark on the 21st.

The Union wanted to seize the important Confederate railroad centers of the region, especially Corinth, Miss., and set up their base of operations at Savannah for the upcoming campaign. The Army of the Ohio under Major General Don Carlos Buell was to join Grant's Army of the Tennessee at this location (near a small church called Shiloh), but the Confederate army of Albert Sidney Johnston planned to attack before Buell could arrive.

Just after 5 a.m. on April 6, Union camps were surprised and overrun by the rebels, and the Federals fought desperately to reorganize against the Confederate onslaught. The Seventh was engaged around 8 a.m. and sent to Duncan Field, adjacent to the Main Corinth Road, just after 9:30 a.m. There, they formed the right flank of the Hornet's Nest defense of W.H.L. Wallace, who had succeeded Smith as the Second Division Commander two weeks before.

The Hornet's Nest was one of the most horrific bastions of the war. Eleven Confederate attacks to take the heavily wooded position were repulsed before the rebels lined up an incredible 62 guns--then the largest concentration of artillery assembled on the continent--to blast the Federal lines. By 4 p.m., the Union defenders finally began to disintegrate, and Rowett saw that the Confederates were attempting to turn his right flank and cut his line of retreat.

With no immediate support for either flank and their .69 caliber ammunition running low, Rowett quickly led his force northeast through thick timber. The enemy forces threatening Rowett helped break the Union lines in the Hornet's Nest, and at 5:30 p.m., the remaining Federals surrendered after a stand that almost transcended human ability.

The Seventh moved to join the lines of Major General John McClernand and fought with those forces for the rest of the day. Rowett's horse was shot from under him during one charge, and the Seventh was part of the repulse of a final enemy thrust. The men slept on their arms that night after an exceptionally bloody day of fighting that almost saw the Union troops driven into the Tennessee River.

Buell's men arrived by steamboat that night, and Grant's advance pushed the enemy back the following day. The Seventh was engaged in hotly contested action again throughout April 7, which finally ended in a Union victory with a staggering cost of life--13,000 Union casualties and 10,700 rebel losses, including their commander, Johnston, shot and killed on April 6. With their defeat, the Confederates were forced to evacuate Tennessee and were further subjected to the threat of Union invasion.

Rowett himself was twice wounded, once in the left breast, but again drew the high compliments of all. Ambrose declared that "no regimental commander handled his command at Shiloh better than Rowett" and that he was always found where danger most threatened. He was sent to a northern hospital to recover from his wounds and eventually went home to Carlinville.

The year of 1862 was proving to be a whirlwind of activity for Rowett, whose military worth helped earn him a promotion to lieutenant colonel dating from April 28. He was fast climbing the ranks, and his personal life took a turn with his marriage that year to the former Emma Brink. It was indeed a full period in the life of Dick Rowett.

He returned to his command on May 18 and participated in the creeping-slow Union advance on Corinth, which was evacuated on May 30. The Seventh then spent time repairing roads and bridges in northern Mississippi before returning to Corinth on June 11. In early July, Babcock, now colonel, returned from leave and assumed command of the Seventh, with Rowett his immediate junior. A few days later, the regiment's colors, torn apart at Fort Donelson and Shiloh, were sent to Springfield and replaced with a new stand.

When the Confederates abandoned Corinth, Memphis was cut off from the east while the important port city of Mobile lost communications from the Tennessee Valley. With the Union eating up more and more of the Mississippi River, the South looked to regain some lost ground. Recapturing Corinth and its vital rail connections would be a major victory to the sagging Southern cause in the West.

Now part of a 21,000-man force under Major General William S. Rosecrans, the Seventh waited out an expected rebel attack from mid-September on. Finally, on October 3, the 22,000 Confederates of Earl Van Dorn struck Rosecrans' somewhat unprepared army, with the weight of the attack falling on the Union center, where the Seventh was located. Following an exhaustive day of fighting, water was in great want, but the only liquid the men could find was a barrel of vinegar from another camp.

The attack resumed the following day in unseasonable ninety-degree heat, with continued intensity along the Union center at Battery Robinett. The Federal lines were battered by heavy fire, and a Union regiment broke and was joined by other fleeing troops. Rowett and Babcock rallied the Seventh and continued as rebel fire opened from the rear, but the men again regrouped and held on. The rear fire had just renewed when, amid the confusion, a Union battery opened a siege gun on their own lines, killing several in the crossfire. Still, the Seventh held, and combat continued for several hours before the assault deteriorated and Van Dorn was driven off in retreat.

The Confederates lost 4,838 men to Rosecrans' 2,839, while Rowett was wounded once again. He was praised anew from his superiors for his gallantry and his efforts in securing the breaks in the lines. He had fought in three intense battles in only a few months with exemplary performance. The year had been unforgiving, and better times did not lay ahead.

IV
Valiant Officer

Rowett and the Seventh Illinois received their indoctrination into war in Tennessee and Mississippi in 1862, but no major fighting would follow for months. Instead, the men received more firsthand experience in the misery of Civil War camp life.

For much of the upcoming months, the Seventh Illinois was stationed around Corinth and in western Tennessee, serving on garrison duty while scouting, foraging, and capturing any Confederates they could find. "Confiscation and extermination" became the unofficial motto of the foraging missions that attempted to weaken the region while sustaining their own war effort. But it was not long before monotony and boredom set in as the war dragged on through the harsh winter of 1862-63.

It was particulary hard in early January as the garrison, cut off from communications for over two weeks, was forced into half rations while facing the winter cold. When supplies did finally arrive, the mail did not come with them--depriving the miserable soldiers of any contact from home. Combined with the boredom of unsanitary, crowded camps, it made life difficult for the heroes trying to win a filthy, atrocious war.

Since the mail was irregular at best, it is unclear when Rowett received the news that he had become a father with the birth of a son on January 14, 1863. Named Richard Rosecrans Rowett--presumably for the Union commander--the word no doubt eased the suffering of camp life; but it also probably made Rowett even more anxious for a quick end to the conflict.

Although Rowett was not able to build on his already growing reputation in battle, his character may be seen in the daily episodes of life on the front. On one scouting mission shortly after the battle of Corinth, Rowett and the Seventh were returning from a scouting mission when they passed a sweet potato patch--a welcome sight to men sick of bacon, hardtack, and other tiresome rations. In a display of dark humor, Rowett sent the men into the patch, commanding them to go to work or he would buck and gag them. "With a gusto," Ambrose wrote, the men quickly dug up potatoes enough to fill their haversacks and "enjoyed a bountiful supper" that evening.

In April, the Seventh was ordered into northern Alabama for more scouting and garrison duties, pleasing the bored soldiers, who were happy to finally have something else to do. Several days were spent in the Tuscumbia Valley and along the Bear River, where Rowett--now colonel and commander of the Seventh, dating to February 28--established himself as an annoyance to the Confederate guerilla cause, especially the brigade of Phillip Roddey, a former sheriff and steamboat man who spent much of the war wreaking havoc along the Tennessee River. Roddey would become a very familiar opponent of the Seventh as the war progressed.

Late that month, the Seventh was trying to cross the swollen Bear River, and men were ordered to swim the river and protect others that were to follow on rafts. Major General Grenville Dodge, the division commander, approached Rowett and asked if his men could swim, to which the hardy Rowett replied, "General, I would not have a man that could not swim." Against a severe current, the men plunged in, and soon were on the opposite bank--except for one soldier, a poor swimmer who, fearing shame and discharge, attempted the crossing in heed of Rowett's declaration to Dodge and nearly drowned in doing so. Rowett, in recognition of the dangerous effort, did not banish the man, seeing that he had the courage to try.

In May, the Seventh returned to Tennessee for more garrison duty, and the next month was mounted on mules on order of Dodge. This directive was not well received by the proud men of the veteran Seventh, who struggled in breaking the stubborn animals as the men soon learned of the mules' "spring towards the latter end" and were "elevated" by the kicking beasts. After considerable effort, the men succeeded in taming the creatures, which consequently led to disagreements of which man had the superior mule. Rowett obviously relished the mounting of the Seventh, as he knew that he could give more rein to his horse, Bay Charley, on upcoming marches.

The adventures of Charley were also the stuff of legend. Rowett found the horse early in the war in a Kentucky cave, hidden in an apparent attempt to keep him from the advancing Federals. Quickly recognized by Rowett to be a thoroughbred, Charley would carry him throughout the war and often helped his master escape danger. Once, Charley walked a single plank of a bridge blown up by the rebels, helping Rowett to safety when the enemy feared to pursue. On another occasion, Rowett was reconnoitering in mountainous territory when rebels cut him off, but he escaped by jumping Charley across a broad chasm. For all of his courage, Rowett could thank Charley for saving his life in more than one instance.

****

Both the men of the Seventh and their mules took it on the chin at a plantation near Purdy, where they surrounded the home a known rebel guerilla in an attempt to capture him. Finding no such man at home, the regiment set up camp for the night on the plantation grounds and, not unexpectedly, raided the corn pens, gardens, and chicken coops for food.

That infuriated the family at home, including an older female head of the household, who called the men all sorts of names before grabbing a hoe and driving them from the yard. She then set about beating on the mules before seeing Rowett pass through the yard, and she immediately went after him with the hoe, screaming that "you, the leader of these vandals, clear out of my yard." As Ambrose mused, the affable Rowett succeeded in quieting the old woman and, somehow, persuaded her to give him his supper. Obviously, the "leader of the vandals" came out well in the matter.

Rowett's personality combined with his fearlessness and

bravery to endear him to his men, who seemingly worshipped their 33-year-old commander as he led them across western Tennessee and northern Mississippi. It may have been a dirty, lonesome war, but Rowett found some pleasure in it; he took great pride in his command, and the leadership ability that would help him in later years was clearly evident. As an admiring Ambrose wrote in November 1863, Rowett "never seems more in his element than when on Charley, thundering over the hills and through the ravines of Tennessee. There is always power felt where he moves."

By then, the fortunes of war had changed in both the Eastern and Western theaters with events only days apart in July. The massive Union victory at Gettysburg gave the North momentum that it would not relinquish, and the fall of Vicksburg, the last major port on the Mississippi, on July 4 gave the Federals control of that major waterway. Federal campaigns continued to gnaw away at Confederate territory as 1863 wore on, and the rebels were about to be driven from Tennessee by year's end. Morale in the North improved, and more favored the continuation of the war until the South succumbed.

Things were not as rosy back in Macoupin County, however. The Copperhead influence remained as strong as ever, and vigilante groups like the Knights of the Golden Circle threatened the security of pro-Union citizens around Carlinville. The fearsome anti-Union sentiment disturbed the men on the front; no doubt Rowett was troubled with the problems at home and Palmer, now major general and commander of the XIV Corps of the Army of the Cumberland, felt in mid-1863 that the enemy at home were as disloyal and dangerous as the enemy in the field.

But, on the front, the mood of the soldiers also lagged. The end of the three-year terms was approaching, and a great number of homesick men were tired of fighting and marching in a war that never seemed to end. Even the Seventh--the first unit to go to war and one of the most respected--had many men who doubted that they would re-enlist.

Although the threat of men going home never became a serious problem, Congress passed the Veteran Volunteer Act, which gave any soldier who re-enlisted a month-long furlough, transportation home, and a $400 bounty. The act induced many soldiers to sign up again, and regiments started heading home on furlough early in 1864.

The Seventh was likely the first to return, but did so in an unusually boisterous manner, getting into an altercation with provost guards on the train home and facing discipline as a result. However, the excitement of the men anxious to see home after a long absence is understandable, even in the case of honored regiments like the Seventh.

Their return to Springfield on January 18 set off a wild welcome that included an emotional march through town and an address by Governor Richard Yates at the state house. Rowett also was called to speak, and he thanked the crowd for their enthusiastic reception and briefly mentioned his and the regiment's renewal to fighting for the Union cause. He closed by urging the soldiers to be ready to return in thirty days and warned the men to keep away from low places and go home like soldiers to see their friends while they had the opportunity.

Thirty days passed all too quickly for many of the men, and they left Camp Butler for Pulaski, Tenn. on February 18. Rowett, though, did not join them, for he had been assigned by special order to the command of Camp Butler.

Being in charge of this important training and prisoner-of-war facility did not appeal to Rowett, who longed for his former command on the front. After several weeks, his request to return to the Seventh was granted, and he reported to his old post at its headquarters in Florence, Ala. on April 8.

There, the Seventh again was charged with eliminating the threat of rebel guerrillas as Roddey was up to his old tricks along the Tennessee. The Confederate commander crossed the river with a motive to defeat Rowett, whose troopers had caused him a year's worth of troubles. Now in charge of the Seventh as well as the

Ninth Ohio Cavalry Volunteers, Rowett stayed busy for weeks staving off Roddey's threat.

On May 7, Roddey attacked companies of the Seventh posted at Florence and Sweetwater and, after a six hour fight, succeeded in driving off the Federals, taking over thirty prisoners. Rowett found himself in a tenous position against the swarming rebels after the skirmish, and he fought desperately to protect a wagon train of supplies that was directed out of Florence. Delicate maneuvering followed in the next couple of days as Rowett directed his men from Pulaski into northern Alabama before coming back across the state line to Prospect.

But the rebels were relentless, and Rowett soon learned of their plans to head off the Union command and burn a large railroad bridge that spanned the Elk River at Prospect. Fearing the loss of the bridge, Rowett and his command swam the Elk against a swift current during a terrible storm on the night of May 10, reaching the sparsely guarded bridge in time to save it the next morning. Rowett's fearlessness knew no limits when Union interests were threatened.

On May 15, Rowett advanced on a small rebel force near Centre Star, capturing a dozen prisoners, and Roddey crossed the Tennessee River the next day, apparently giving up the goal of driving Rowett from northern Alabama. Once again, there was peace--relatively speaking--in the region.

The Seventh spent much of the next month patrolling along the Tennessee until June 14, when the regiment was dismounted, ordered to Chattanooga, and eventually sent to Tilton, Ga. as part of the massive campaign on the venerable Confederate stronghold of Atlanta. The Seventh, part of the XV Corps of the Army of the Tennessee, joined the Armies of the Cumberland and the Ohio, a force 100,000 strong under William Tecumseh Sherman, who squared off against Joseph Johnston's Army of Tennessee in a brilliant series of maneuvers that lasted from May 1864 until autumn.

Two weeks passed as the Seventh performed duties similar

to those they had known for two years, guarding railroads, hunting guerrillas, and the like. On July 29, the three-year veterans who did not re-enlist were mustered out, among them Joseph, who had risen to the rank of first lieutenant when he was discharged.

Rowett was no doubt sorry to lose his brother and close companion, but the reasons for Joe's departure may have went beyond merely being ready to quit fighting. Problems in Dick's household in Carlinville that would come to a head late in 1864 may well have been festering at that time, and one may speculate that Joe returned to look after things, like his brother's 18-month-old son.

But the war went on, and on August 15 Rowett assumed command of the Third Brigade of the Fourth Division of XV Corps, which included his own Seventh, the 50th and 57th Illinois Infantry, and the 39th Iowa Infantry. Scouting and foraging activities continued from the brigade's headquarters at Rome, Ga. while Sherman's forces closed in on Atlanta and exposed the recklessness of John Bell Hood, who had relieved the much-maligned Johnston on July 17.

The Confederates finally evacuated Atlanta on September 1, and Federal troops occupied the city the next morning to conclude months of skirmishing and flanking movements in a hard-won victory. However, Hood marched northward to threaten Sherman's communication lines to Chattanooga in an attempt to draw Sherman northward and force him to abandon Atlanta as the mood of the war in Georgia remained tense throughout the fall of 1864.

Richard Rowett, probably late in the war. (Courtesy of the Illinois State Historical Library)

V
Allatoona

Hood's massive diversionary tactic led the Army of Tennessee north out of Atlanta to destroy Sherman's communication lines while capturing garrison troops left to guard those lines. His immediate plan was to draw Sherman northward, forcing him to abandon Atlanta, but that was only part of a grander plan--to invade Tennessee, retake Nashville, and perhaps continue into Kentucky.

It was a risky plan, at best. Hood's tired army was greatly weakened from losses suffered around Atlanta, and he was running desperately short of supplies. Superiors disapproved of the plan, but the reckless Hood embarked on it anyway in the hopes of changing the fortunes of the war in the West.

Hood remained at Lovejoy, 25 miles south of Atlanta, until September 18, when he realized that Sherman was not immediately proceeding to move South. Effective raiding in Tennessee by the notorious Nathan Bedford Forrest forced Sherman to send Major General George Thomas, leader of the Army of the Cumberland, to Nashville, with three divisions to protect that city and Chattanooga. But Thomas did not have enough men to protect against both Hood and Forrest, which forced Sherman to move 55,000 of his troops northward while sending the Fourth Division of Brigadier General John M. Corse (of which Rowett's brigade was a part) to Rome, 50 miles northwest of Atlanta, leaving 12,000 men to guard Atlanta itself and postponing a planned southward invasion. For the moment, Hood had succeeded in diverting Sherman's attention.

Hood was beginning to tear up railroads around Marietta and cause general concern when he learned of a large railroad supply depot that the Federals had established at Allatoona Pass, some twenty miles northwest. The depot held over a million rations of bread and other supplies that were crucial to Sherman's army, and Hood quickly dispatched a division under Major

General Samuel G. French to capture the position.

The advance units of the Federal main forces were reaching Kennesaw Mountain, 13 miles southeast of Allatoona, on October 4 when Sherman learned of French's advance. An 890-man garrison commanded by Lieutenant Colonel John Tourtelotte of the 4th Minnesota was defending Allatoona, and Sherman immediately ordered Corse from Rome to reinforce the garrison.

Corse, a 29-year-old lawyer from Iowa known for his exaggerations and self-dramatization, quickly loaded the 1,054 men of Rowett's Third Brigade, which included the Seventh and 50th Illinois, the 39th Iowa, two companies of the 57th Illinois, and a detachment of the 12th Illinois, and 165,000 rounds of ammunition onto 20 railroad cars and left for Allatoona. They arrived around 1 a.m. on October 5 and Corse immediately sent the train back to Rome for more reinforcements, but the locomotive derailed, cutting off additional help.

Allatoona Pass, the site of some of the maneuvering between Sherman and Johnston that spring, consists of a high, crooked ridge separated by a railroad cut, with fortifications situated on either side of the south end of the ridge. The warehouses were located at the southern foot of the ridge near the cut. Earthworks in equally crooked formation extended from the redoubts, with additional rifle pits and breastworks located in various locations across the ridge. Sharpened stakes placed in front of the lines made an offensive that much more difficult, and the steep slopes created another obstacle.

Corse took over the redoubt to the west (called the "Star Fort" due to its shape), while Tourtelotte set up his position at the fort east of the cut. Rowett, the Seventh, and the 39th Iowa were sent into the lines west of Star Fort as the men slept on their arms in anticipation of an attack.

French made a night march from Ackworth and ran into Federal pickets around the small town of Allatoona around 3 a.m. At 7:30, the Confederate artillery, 12 guns strong, opened fire on the forts as skirmishing began in earnest. French sent one of his brigades, Mississippians under Claudius Sears, to the northeast to get behind the forts and cut railroad and telegraph lines. This action left Corse without communications.

By 8:30, French had positioned his other two brigades to the west of the pass, effectively surrounding the Northerners. The Confederate commander then sent Corse an ultimatum, calling on him to surrender to "avoid a needless effusion of blood." Corse responded in kind, refusing French's demand by saying that "we are prepared for the 'needless effusion of blood' whenever it is agreeable to you."

Although this exchange has become a favorite anecdote of the war, French later wrote that he never received Corse's reply. According to the Confederate commander, his messenger waited over fifteen minutes for an answer from Corse and, not receiving one, returned to headquarters.

The attack followed shortly, with the Seventh and the 39th Iowa in the rifle pits the first to feel the brunt. A brigade of Missourians under Brigadier General Frances M. Cockrell made the first strike and, after the Unionists staved them off, were joined by the Texas brigade of Brigadier General W.H. Young. That charge, too, was beaten back with the help of the sixteen-shooter Henry rifles of the Seventh.

These weapons, technologically advanced at the time, had been purchased by the men of the Seventh themselves, who came up with the purchase price of $50 out of their own pay, a mere $13 a month. Theirs was the only regiment in the entire army to buy their own guns, and the repeating rifles more than paid for themselves against wave after wave of rebel attackers.

Rowett's command held off repeated charges despite heavy losses until late in the morning and was about to be overrun when Sears' brigade swept in from the north. Tourtelotte's men in the east redoubt fired on the Mississippians, breaking up the charge, but the Confederates regrouped and pressed on to the battered rifle pits. This forced Rowett, who had withstood a hailstorm of deadly Confederate fire from three sides for two and

Allatoona Pass. (Reprinted from *Allatoona Pass: A Needless Effusion of Blood* with permission from the author; photo processing by Daugherty Photography, Carlinville, Illinois)

a half hours, to fall back to the Star Fort around 11 a.m.

In the midst of this harrowing retreat, Rowett suffered a shell wound to the leg and was carried into the fort as the Federals fought desperately to reach shelter. A fearless stand by a detachment of the 39th Iowa bought enough time for the rest of the men to pour into the fort, but Colonel James Redfield of the 39th, already wounded three times, was shot through the heart and finally fell, dead.

Chaos reigned inside the fort, but the high command rallied the men sufficiently to continue holding off the Confederate onslaught. Despite his wound, Rowett continued to spur on his men, and Corse sent for reinforcements from the east redoubt.

As the battle intensified, Sherman reached Kennesaw Mountain, where he anxiously viewed the battle through field glasses and waited for news. With communications to Allatoona cut off, Sherman was uncertain if Corse had reinforced Tourtelotte and was unable to decipher any messages via signal flag. Finally, the signal officer made out these letters from another message: 'C,' 'R,' 'S,' 'E,' 'H,' 'E,' 'R.'' The signal officer read this as "Corse is here" and Sherman is said to have shouted, "I understand it! Corse is there all right. He'll hold out. I know the man!"

Sometime during the exchange of signals, the signal officer at Kennesaw Mountain sent Corse this message; "General Sherman says hold fast; we are coming." After the battle, journalists translated the message into "Hold the fort; I am coming." This emphatic statement--although not entirely accurate--captured the imagination of the North, and the words were soon used as the theme of evangelist P.P. Bliss' revival hymn "Hold the Fort." The resulting popularity of the hymn helped ensure Allatoona's place in both history and legend. One later account says that Rowett received the dispatch, although modern historians do not substantiate this.

The Federals, now reinforced with men of the 12th and 50th Illinois regiments, continued their heavy fire from the Star Fort and a ditch extending from the redoubt, but repeated assaults from the Confederates brought them closer and closer. The rebels used everything they could find on the rough ground for protection, crouching behind stumps and logs and ducking into holes and trenches to stay out of the path of Union bullets.

Around 1 p.m., Corse went down with a wound to his face, knocking him senseless for over a half hour. Rowett assumed command of the Union troops, who were running low of ammunition and whose gun barrels were nearly too hot to touch.

All along, the Federals had hoped that reinforcements from Sherman would arrive, and with ammunition in short supply, the situation was tenuous. Rowett ordered the men to conserve what ammunition was left, and cries of "cease firing" ran up and down the lines. This command was misconstrued by some of the men as meaning "surrender," and Corse somehow jumped to his feet, screaming "No surrender, hold Allatoona." Additional ammunition from Tourtelotte's redoubt was sent for and the battle raged on, although there was never any intention of stopping it in the first place.

Around this time, 1:30 p.m., Rowett was felled when a minie ball fractured his skull. Bleeding badly, he soon fainted from the loss of blood, yet another casualty among many the Seventh was incurring as the Confederates tried in vain to take the position.

The offensive began to flicker around 2 p.m., and, seeing that the warehouses could not be won by assault, the Confederates made an unsuccessful attempt to burn them. By 4 p.m., the rebels were too disorganized to attack again, and French had received information that a large Federal force was preparing to cut him off from the main body of Hood's army, located 20 miles to the southwest around Dallas. The information was incorrect as no Union troops were near enough to threaten until the next morning. Still, French ordered a general withdrawal, but not before capturing 84 men of the 18th Wisconsin in a blockhouse at a railroad bridge two miles south.

The Union had held Allatoona, but at a tremendous cost. The defenders lost a total of 707 men of the 1,944 troops of Tourtelotte's garrison and Rowett's reinforcements. French's loss was 799 of slightly over 2,000 engaged, with Young wounded and later captured. Of his defenders, Sherman later said that, "for the numbers engaged, they stood on the bloodiest battlefield ever known upon the American continent." In his definitive 1995 account of the battle, William R. Scaife lists the total losses of the battle at 30% and states that, for the short time of the actual engagement, it was the highest rate incurred in any battle of the war.

Of 299 men, the Seventh lost 35 killed, 67 wounded, and 39 missing--a staggering total of 141 casualties. 170 of the 280 men of the 39th Iowa, who defended the pits with the Seventh, were lost, including Redfield. In a telling number of the ferocity of the firing, the new battle flag of the 12th Wisconsin Artillery was pierced by 192 bullets during the fight.

With his severe head wound, there was doubt as to whether Rowett would survive. Surgeons worked through the night of the battle as the men of the Seventh prayed for his life.

Historians credit Rowett's morning stand in the rifle pits, as well as the delaying action to cover the men during the retreat to the west redoubt, as critical to the successful defense of Allatoona. Rowett himself credited the Henry sixteen-shooters, saying that without the repeating rifles, the Union forces would have been overwhelmed.

Some have said that, had the Union lost Allatoona and its valuable stores, it is unlikely that Sherman could have embarked on his intention of a march to the sea. Sherman had been trying to convince Grant and the high command in Washington of the merits of his plan, and the fall of Allatoona may well have ended his hopes. For its relatively small size--only a total of 4,000 men were engaged on both sides--the fame and legend of Allatoona is

seemingly endless and greater than many larger engagements.
Rowett's role at Allatoona won him recognition in much-lauded historical sources. He is credited in the landmark work *Abraham Lincoln: A History* by Lincoln's personal secretaries, John Hay and John Nicolay, and Sherman makes complimentary mention of Rowett in his memoirs. Ambrose, of course, writes glowingly of Rowett's bravery, and subsequent regimental histories of the 50th and 93rd Illinois both speak highly of him.

Sherman, no doubt happy with the defense of his stores, issued a general order on October 7 in praise of the battle.

The general commanding avails himself of the opportunity, in the handsome defense made at Allatoona, to illustrate the most important principle in war, that fortified posts should be defended to the last, regardless of the relative numbers of the party attacking and attacked...The thanks of this army are due and are hereby accorded to General Corse, Colonel Tourtelotte, Colonel Rowett, officers and men, for their determined and gallant defense of Allatoona, and it is made an example to illustrate the importance of preparing in time, and meeting the danger, when presented, boldly, manfully, and well.

Commanders and garrisons of the posts along our railroads are hereby instructed that they must hold their posts to the last minute, sure that the time gained is valuable and necessary to their comrades at the front.

By order of Major General W.T. Sherman,
L.M. Dayton, Aide-de-Camp

Corse, elated with the defense, on October 6 sent Sherman this message: "I am short a cheekbone and an ear, but am able to whip all hell yet!" When Sherman later saw Corse, he was wearing a bandage on his cheek from being grazed there, but there was hardly any damage to the ear he claimed to have lost. Laughing, Sherman exclaimed, "Corse, they came damned near missing you, didn't they?"

The message demonstrates Corse's self-laudatory manner, and in later years the Rowett family and others would criticize

Corse for claiming the lion's share of the glory of Allatoona. In an 1890 publication on the battle for which Corse was interviewed, he made scarce mention of Rowett or, for that matter, any other officer. In his own memoirs, French takes Corse to task for perceived exaggerations in battle reports and conduct, and the history of the 93rd Illinois reprehends in diplomatic fashion Corse's message to Sherman of October 6. Corse, a leading player in Massachusetts Democratic politics after the war, indeed deserves much praise for his actions at Allatoona, but he was hardly alone in his valor.

****

Hood advanced northward in his continued attempt to draw Sherman away from Atlanta, and Sherman shelved his march to Savannah for the rest of the month. By early November, though, Sherman left Thomas to deal with Hood in Tennessee, and, after finally receiving the go-ahead, started for Savannah on November 15. While the Seventh joined Sherman in the epic march across Georgia, Rowett was left behind in his struggle to regain his health in the face of his severe wounds.

The shot to the left top of his skull caused partial paralysis in his lower extremities and hindered the sight in his right eye, while doctors said his other wound affected his spinal column. Several pieces of bone were removed and a silver plate was inserted into his skull, but the corresponding right side of his body always troubled him, and he walked with a limp for the rest of his life. He never fully recovered from his injuries.

After a stay at the corps field hospital, Rowett was sent on to an officers' hospital in Nashville before returning home on leave on November 7. He was granted the opportunity to apply for an extension of his leave of absence, which he later did as his recovery lagged.

During this time, his problems went far beyond his wounds. His marriage of two years had failed, and Rowett was granted a divorce from Emma on December 21. Custody of their son, just shy of two years old, went to the father.

Divorce in the mid-19th century was rare, and for custody to be awarded to the father was even more unusual. The court considered sworn evidence from a witness as well as the contents of certain letters, and they concluded as aforementioned. It is easy to speculate that Emma had been unfaithful to the marriage, but there is no proof of this.

Now a single father, Rowett took care of things at home and did whatever he could for the Seventh, including a trip to Springfield early in 1865 to raise recruits. While he was away, a petition was circulated among the officers of the Third Brigade recommending Rowett for promotion to brigadier general. Interestingly, the petition was strongly backed by Corse.

By then, the North was controlling the outcome of the rebellion, as Grant's ongoing siege of Petersburg was choking Lee while Sherman had turned north from Savannah and was laying even greater waste to South Carolina. The South was collapsing under extreme inflation, widespread shortages, and an ever-increasing lack of men as the grand cause was dying away. The Confederates continued to hold slim hopes of a turn in the tide of the conflict, but when Petersburg (and, subsequently, Richmond) fell on April 2, it was not to be. The once-proud Army of Northern Virginia, now a ragged, half-starved lot of largely unarmed men, surrendered at Appomattox Court House on April 9, and the remaining Confederates were soon to follow.

By April, Rowett's arduous recovery had progressed enough for him to reassume command of his brigade. It is likely that, while on his way to join Sherman's army in North Carolina, he heard the news of the assassination of President Lincoln. The joy that came with Lee's surrender was fleeting; the great man who had presided over the nation's darkest hours was shot only five days later, and died the following morning. For a nation wrought with four years of warfare, the news was too much to bear and deep mourning reigned, even in the defeated South.

Sherman was meeting with Johnston, who had returned to replace Hood as commander of the decimated Army of Tennessee in February, to discuss surrender on April 17 when he learned of the

news of the assassination. Both men, shaken by the news, signed a treaty that was vetoed in Washington, and a revised plan was signed on April 26.

Rowett returned to his old command at Morrisville, North Carolina on April 20, only days before the army left on its northward march to Washington for the Grand Review on May 24. By then, Rowett had his stars; effective to March 13, he was brevetted brigadier general for gallant conduct at Allatoona on the recommendation of Sherman. From his beginning as captain of the Carlinville Invincibles, the hero of Allatoona would be known as General Rowett.

From Washington, the Seventh was ordered to Louisville, Ky. and later served provost guard duty. On July 9, 1865, the regiment was mustered out of service and sent on to Springfield, arriving on July 11 and spending a week there before the men were paid off and discharged. The role of the Seventh, the first to serve from Illinois and one of the best, in the most horrifying period of American history was complete.

On Previous Page:
Top: General officers of the Fourth Division, taken in May 1865. Rowett is seated at left, followed by William Thomas Clarke, John M. Corse, and Elliott Warren Rice. (Massachusetts Commandery Military Order of the Loyal Legion and United States Army Military History Institute, Carlisle Barracks, Pa.)

Bottom: Rowett with officers of the Seventh Illinois Volunteer Infantry. He is seated in the second row, third from the right. Among the other officers in the picture is Brig. Gen. John Cook, seated at Rowett's right. (Roger D. Hunt Collection, United States Army Military History Institute, Carlisle Barracks, Pa.)

VI
Returning War Hero

Dick Rowett returned to Carlinville after the war, and, like his fellow veterans, received a hero's welcome. But his glory was surprisingly short-lived.

To honor its "boys in blue," Carlinville planned a town meeting and an elaborate picnic, complete with a soldiers' march in military dress. Rowett was appointed marshal of the military for the August 24 celebration, with all soldiers to report to him to form the procession.

The march, intended to be an orderly, dignified exhibition, turned out to be a lighthearted stroll in which the men, many in civillian's clothing, were more concerned with the admiring young ladies than with military order. The citizens of Carlinville turned out *en masse* in a warm display of pride for their veteran neighbors.

Many veterans across the nation hoped that pride would carry them to political office. It was just a month beyond the final muster-out of the men, but even in Macoupin County, there was a movement to send their top soldiers into the high county offices.

The night before the picnic, the Union County Convention, a group composed largely of soldiers of the rebellion, met at the courthouse to elect a ticket for the upcoming county campaigns. This group, in essence a Republican outlet, supported the policies of Lincoln's successor, Andrew Johnson, and honored all soldiers while hoping to build a permanent monument to those fallen men at a cost of $5,000-$10,000. With this obvious platform, the convention put in soldiers as candidates for all major county offices, with Rowett receiving the nod for county clerk.

In a nation high with emotion over the late war, the Union ticket may have seemed a lock to carry the November elections, but Macoupin County was still heavily Democratic. The Copperhead sentiment of the war had not faded out, for many Macoupinites still did not favor the war or the principles of the victorious North.

Due in part to this dissent and in part to the passion of the day, elections of even the smallest scale were vicious, bitter, and piercing. Elections that appear dirty today pale in comparison to the personal attacks and mockery that ruled campaigns in nineteenth-century America. It was no different in Carlinville, where the two newspapers squared off on even the most insignificant of issues.

Rowett was soon bombarded from every possible angle in the Democratic *Spectator*, who hardly gave the General time to enjoy his nomination before questioning "why and where he got his stars" and implying that they were trumped up to "catch soldiers' votes." The *Free Democrat*, in turn, blasted the *Spectator* for its hard-line anti-war stance and its editor for, among other things, his "traitorous heart" and his "cowardly instincts."

After several weeks of enduring the wrath of the *Spectator*, Rowett invited the editor of that paper, J.R. Flynn, to meet him in a debate in Chesterfield on Saturday evening, October 14. A sizable crowd of partisans attended the event, including the *Free Democrat*, who wrote that "not much was expected of Flynn; everyone knew he could not be wise, but his friends fondly hoped he might prove to be witty." Even that, according to the *Free Democrat*, was not enough, chortling that "Flynn, as a wit, would have excited pity, had he commanded sufficient respect as a man."

Rowett came well-prepared and proceeded to discredit Flynn at every opportunity, repeatedly referring to back issues of the *Spectator* to embarrass its editor. The General later produced a copy of the oath of the Knights of the Golden Circle in the handwriting of the Democratic candidate for assessor, who was in the crowd and quickly confessed. Flynn, also exposed, followed his confession as Rowett came away with a resounding victory in the debate, much to the glee of the *Free Democrat*.

Despite the best efforts of Rowett and the *Free Democrat*, the campaign still proved to be an uphill battle. The incumbent, George H. Holliday, was a wealthy banker and one-time owner of the *Spectator* and had enjoyed a substantial political career of his own. Holliday and Rowett met in a series of public appearances across the county as the election neared.

Rowett no doubt proved worthy in his public speaking. A fine orator with a forceful voice and eloquent approach, he was able, it was said, to "whoop 'em up at political rallies in a most appealing fashion." For years, he would remain a stalwart of Macoupin Republicanism and was a featured speaker at numerous county rallies and functions.

But it was still not enough to win the race. Rowett carried only eight of 23 townships and collected 2,208 votes to Holliday's 2,605, winning less than forty-six percent of the vote. Macoupin had voted twice against Lincoln and now sent the soldiers to defeat in another display of the power of the local Democracy. Rowett may have won Allatoona, but he could not win over the voters of Macoupin County.

The *Free Democrat*, of course disgusted with the outcome, still had the last word. Two weeks after the election, the paper reported that Rowett's war horse, Charley, "again distanced all competitors" at the local races on Saturday, November 18, writing that the "General's exchequer was strengthened $500 or more by the operation." All told, said the *Free Democrat*, it was "rather more profitable than running for Court House stakes."

****

One of the issues raised in the 1865 elections, although not necessarily in the race for county clerk, was the building of a new Macoupin County courthouse. In 1867, the state legislature authorized the county commissioners to raise funds for the proposed new building, the cost of which was said to be $50,000 but in no event should have exceeded $75,000.

The plan for the new building was said to be in response to fears that Macoupin County would be divided into two smaller counties and that Carlinville would not be the county seat of either.

Others have said that the residents of the county and the county court simply needed a new, larger courthouse building. Rumors that Macoupin County would be annexed to its neighbor to the north, Sangamon County, were also circulating, and it has also been speculated that the planners wanted Carlinville to become the capital of Illinois and needed a sufficient building for that purpose. It is more likely that the fears of county division, as well as the supposed need for a larger building, were the actual reasons.

But the costs of such a grandiose, majestic building were higher than any citizen could have imagined. From the original estimates of $50,000, by January 1869 it was reported that $449,604 had been paid out and the building was still not close to completion.

Sole authority of this project was in the hands of a commission of four, including Holliday, county justice Isham J. Peebles, county judge T.L. Loomis (the agent for the county with absolute powers), and A. McKim DuBois, whose firm sold the bonds for the building. To pay for it all, taxes were to be levied, and for a rural county of 32,305 residents, the burden was too great for reasonable people to bear.

As early as 1867, citizens were screaming "taxation without representation," and opposition grew over the next two years to a fever pitch. The court pressed on, though, sending agents to Springfield in February 1869 to present its case to the legislature and work for the passage of a bill "legalizing certain acts of the county court to complete the courthouse," including borrowing more money and raising more taxes.

This incensed the taxpayers, who were outraged at this latest attempt to railroad the courthouse through at all costs. Two leading Carlinville lawyers and politicians, General John I. Rinaker and C.A. Walker, argued that completion of the building as planned would result in taxes that would almost be confiscatory. They also discovered that some of the numbers on the courthouse bonds had been duplicated, causing even further protests of misdeed.

A mass meeting was called in Carlinville on February 23, 1869 to protest the bill, which had passed in the Senate and was pending in the House. The large crowd in attendance that night included Rowett, who spoke against the proposed legislation at the meeting. Eventually, he was one of 25 citizens, including Rinaker, Walker, and H.M. Kimball, editor of the *Democrat*, appointed at the meeting to work for the defeat of the bill in Springfield.

There, the group appeared before the Judiciary Committee, armed with petitions of thousands of taxpayers urging defeat of the bill. The commissioners for the courthouse also made a presentation to the Judiciary Committee, saying that, despite altered plans for the building, the cost would not be more than $500,000. On March 9, the Judiciary Committee recommended passage of the bill. No limits were set on the county court to borrow money, although the concerns of the citizens were recognized in the recommendation.

Finally, in 1870, the new courthouse was completed. After original estimates for a new courthouse were $50,000, the elaborate design, coupled with financial mismanagement and lofty expectations, had blown the final cost to a staggering $1,380,500.

The backlash of the controversy was felt immediately. All of the commissioners, especially Loomis and Holliday, were harshly criticized for their roles in pushing the building through. They were not in office to see completion of the courthouse, as a new court was elected by an angry public in the 1869 campaign. Due in large part to the controversy, Macoupin County adopted township government in 1871 to prevent a few men acting without regard to the multitudes.

Now in disgrace, Holliday boarded a train out of Carlinville in 1870 and was never heard from again. He was later indicted by a grand jury for larceny and embezzlement, and as many as fifteen separate indictments were reached before the case was stricken from the docket with leave to reinstate. Undoubtedly, Rowett must have felt at least some satisfaction at the demise of his old opponent.

A man of modest wealth himself, Rowett was long known as an advocate of the common man. He had seen how the taxes generated by the courthouse would crush the taxpayers, and he took a stand. Had he been elected county clerk, or had other members of his ticket been elected, it is likely that the present courthouse would have never been built, or at least reached its massive levels. The same would be true had the Judiciary Committee ruled in favor of Rowett and the citizens.

In that, it is probably just as well that Rowett failed on both counts. The animosity toward the courthouse dissipated with time, and today the Macoupin County Courthouse is the centerpiece of Carlinville. The overwhelming structure is one of the most recognizable landmarks of the region and is toured by hundreds of people every year. The courthouse has long been, and will continue to be, a source of tremendous pride to the residents of Carlinville and Macoupin County. Rowett was not a success as a politician early on and in hindsight, it is better that way.

Macoupin County's "Million-Dollar Courthouse." (Photo by author)

VII
Political Aspirations

While his stint in local politics was unspectacular, Rowett gained recognition and respect in the political arena beyond Carlinville and Macoupin County. And he had friends in high places to help him along.

His allies started at the top of Illinois government. In the 1868 elections, Palmer had swept into the Governor's mansion on the strength of his "bloody shirt" war speeches and his politically moderate Republican beliefs, aided by the current state of upheaval in Illinois politics. Friends before the war, Palmer and Rowett were aligned on the slavery issue, but they were divided over the courthouse, which had the Governor's support. Palmer's repeated changes in political party would distance Rowett in future years, but the two men nonetheless maintained a close friendship.

A month after his inauguration--and ten days before the mass meeting of courthouse opposition--Palmer appointed Rowett as state trustee of the famed Illinois-and-Michigan Canal on February 13, 1869. This waterway, linking Lake Michigan with the Illinois River, was overseen by a committee of three trustees that represented both the state and the bondholders of the canal. While in office, Rowett helped control the financial affairs and maintenance of the canal before the close of the trust in September 1871, when the state assumed responsibility of the canal.

Even before the close of the trust, it was expected that Rowett would receive another assignment in state government. Rowett's good work was augmented by having Palmer in the Governor's chair, and he was named to the three-member board of penitentiary commissioners in 1871.

The penitentiary, located in Joliet, was at that time the sole correctional facility of its kind in the state. The position kept Rowett in the Chicagoland surroundings that he knew as canal trustee, but a leading issue during his tenure was the proposal to build another penitentiary in southern Illinois. He remained in the position until the mid-1870s.

While the nation was once again united and Reconstruction tried to close the wounds of the war, the political scene in the United States was still unsettled, and Illinois was no exception. The presidential administrations of Johnson and Grant came under severe attack on ethical issues, and both the Republican and Democrat parties dealt with dissension as emotions flared on personal and political matters. As was the case before the war, it was not long before groups splintered from the established parties in attempts to form their own political and social machines.

Rowett, up to that time a loyal Republican, himself developed concerns of his party and in 1872 began to align himself with a minority movement that came of opposition to the Grant administration.* Known as the Liberal Republican party, it set about to end widespread corruption in the Grant presidency and alleged despotic treatment of Southerners while reforming civil service and the tariff.

The liberal branch, although new, quickly attracted many influential members of the traditional Republican party, including Palmer, who refused what some believed to be certain renomination for Governor and broke from the Republicans over his disapproval of Grant and national party policies. Other leading Illinoisans who switched to the liberal movement were three-term U.S. Senator Lyman Trumbull and U.S. Supreme Court Justice David Davis, an old friend of Lincoln who declared that Grant was "weak, ignorant, mercenary, selfish, and malignant." The surprisingly high representation of Liberal Republicans in Illinois was echoed in other states, with the support of such media as the *New York Tribune* and the *Chicago Tribune*.

The liberals held their convention in Cincinnati on May 1, 1872 in what was a hodgepodge of ex-Republicans, various Democrats, and current and former subscribers of virtually every political philosophy in the nation. The well-represented Illinois delegation was divided in its support of Presidential candidates, as Rowett stumped for Palmer, while Trumbull and Davis were also in the running. The convention eventually nominated Horace Greeley, the former abolitionist from New York, who also earned the Democrats' nod for President. Rowett, an admirer of Greeley, supported his ticket in the upcoming campaign.

The Republicans nominated Grant again, and he won re-election as the Liberal Republican movement lost its early momentum and quickly died out. Some of those who split from the Republicans paid the price; Palmer's political career stalled after his defection, while Trumbull did not return to the Senate as his career also suffered. Rowett was more fortunate in his return to the Republicans, but he still looked for a more satisfying political outlet.

He was not alone. Political confusion was still prevalent as the mid-1870s approached, and party lines were still ragged and ill-defined with a strong disposition to create new movements. All of this combined in the birth of the Illinois State Reform Party, a fledgling group that met in Springfield on June 10, 1874 in what was described as a collection of "farmers, mechanics, laboring men, and other citizens."

This group, also known as the Farmers' Convention, opposed what it believed to be oppressive monopolies in contemporary politics while arguing for reforms in monetary laws, civil serivce, and patents, in addition to protection of railroad legislation. Rowett was part of the Macoupin County delegation, while Palmer, ever the political opportunist, delivered an impromptu address.

Such gatherings were often emotional and heated, and the Farmers' Convention was certainly that. Rowett helped create much of the tension, starting with his resolution demanding a national return to a uniform standard of value. He warmly defended his resolution, but much confusion erupted, and the General was declared out of order and told to take his seat.

Later, a hot discussion on a resolution for the nation to pay its debts in good faith as the pledges of the country required had just calmed down when Rowett jumped in to argue that the government should pay its debts in accordance with pledges to creditors who had loaned money for the war effort. This re-ignited the discussion, and, as the *Illinois State Journal* reported, "all was tumult."

The hot-tempered Rowett also caused a stir when General William B. Anderson of Jefferson County spoke against those who thought the national debts should be paid in gold, rather than currency. Rowett, who had earlier fought for a uniform standard of value, jumped to his feet and demanded if any reference had been made of him by Anderson. The *Journal* reported that Anderson denied any such reference, and "there was peace again."

The convention submitted nominations for the state elections in the fall, but did not attract a significant number of voters and, like the Liberal Republicans, faded away. Rowett again stayed with the Republicans and in 1876 found himself a candidate for Illinois state representative of the 40th District.

Three seats were available from the district, which covered Macoupin and Jersey counties. The General was one of four candidates in a race that included Hampton Wall, a young Macoupin County Democrat from Staunton running for his first term in the state legislature; John N. English, an elder statesman of Jersey County Democratic politics and a member of the state legislature from 1861-65; and fellow Jersey County politican Oliver P. Powell, who was seeking a return trip to the House as an independent.

Although Republicans had been elected governor in Illinois since 1857 and had controlled the Illinois legislature since 1865, Macoupin County remained a Democratic stronghold, and the elections of Wall and English were nearly guaranteed. Local politics were still very partisan, and the newspapers attacked as viciously as ever; the *Democrat* stayed true to its Republican support, while the *Macoupin Enquirer* (formerly the *Spectator*) attacked Rowett on a regular basis. In response to the *Democrat*'s fears that Powell would be elected, the *Enquirer* retorted that Rowett would be "left out in the cold, which would be a good thing." Later, on another issue, the *Enquirer* reported that "Rowett was blubbering all over the county," and in response to several Rowett appearances in Montgomery County, the *Enquirer* "for his benefit, reminded him that the district in which he is running is composed of the counties of Macoupin and Jersey."

But the General was a highly recognizable figure, and his forceful eloquence in speaking helped him win even greater respect. He campaigned vigorously across the district and ended up with the highest vote total of the four candidates, carrying both Macoupin and Jersey counties with 13,410.5 total votes. Rowett's strong showing may be attributed to his personal popularity as well as his commanding presence and leadership ability.

Rowett took his seat in the 30th General Assembly the following January in Springfield and, as always, became a leading member of that body. His background as penitentiary commissioner no doubt helped him win the chair of the House Penitentiary Committee, and he also served as chair of the South Park Investigation Committee, which examined improprieties among the park commissioners of the city of Chicago.

While in office, Rowett also pushed for additional means to repair sidewalks in cities, towns, and villages, while also arguing for provisions of health and safety for coal miners. Election of a United States Senator was also on the docket in the 30th General Assembly, and Rowett voted for a second term for John A. Logan over the Democratic nominee, old friend Palmer.

Rowett did not seek re-election to the legislature, but he remained a major player in state Republican politics. A regular at state conventions, he was particularly active at the 1880 convention, which was bitterly divided as many, despite his shortcomings in office, wanted to return Grant to the White House over the fervent support of James G. Blaine of Maine. Another key issue at the gathering was the selection of delegates to the national convention; in the past, delegates from the individual congressional districts nominated delegates, but a proposal was made by the Grant men for the convention president to appoint a committee to name delegates.

Rowett, an earnest Grant supporter, steadfastly argued for the proposed change, which would have insured that the Illinois delegation would vote solidly for Grant; under the old way, Blaine supporters would have likely filtered the delegation. The Grant men won out and Rowett himself was named a national delegate, but his seat was contested in a power struggle between the presidential factions that carried over to the national convention. Although he did not support incumbent Shelby Cullom for governor, Rowett had the last word as the votes slipped away, and he moved for unanimous renomination.

As at the state convention, the national convention in Chicago was torn apart over the presidential nomination, while the contesting delegates from ten districts of Illinois were admitted after a prolonged, hostile debate. Rowett was one of anywhere from 302 to 309 delegates who voted for Grant on every ballot in what broke down into a gruelling two-day affair to name a candidate. In their stand, they became known as the "306" who held out for Grant and, in doing so, were remembered for decades. Finally, the Blaine support shifted to James A. Garfield, who locked up the nomination on the 36th ballot.

****

As the years passed, Rowett continued to strengthen ties to some of the leading state and national figures of the day. He corresponded with Robert Todd Lincoln, eldest son of the late President and Secretary of War from 1881-85, and became a friend of politician and great thinker Robert Ingersoll. But, as with Palmer in the Senate voting, friendships never got in the way of politics.

One of Rowett's cohorts was General Green B. Raum, a lawyer, railroad man, and U.S. Representative from 1867-69. Born and raised in Pope County, Raum had commanded the 56th Illinois and presided over the 1880 state convention, where Rowett was named a national delegate. Raum was a candidate for U.S. Senator at a Republican caucus in 1883, and Rowett campaigned for him in a losing cause to Cullom, the Illinois political icon. Although Rowett worked against the venerable Cullom at least twice, they remained on cordial terms, and Cullom spoke highly of the General following his death.

When Logan died in his third term in the Senate on December 26, 1886, Raum was again a candidate for the vacant seat, but Rowett worked for Charles B. Farwell of Chicago, a four-time U.S. Representative who had backed Blaine in 1880. Farwell prevailed on the second ballot.

Rowett was a close ally of Logan himself in an unusual mix of personalities. Logan, a Vice-Presidential candidate in 1884, was Rowett's corps commander late in the war. One of the organizers of the Grand Army of the Republic, Logan also began the observance of Memorial Day, although many--including Palmer--accused the flamboyant southern Illinoisan not only of vanity but also of Southern sympathies before the war.

Logan could always count on Rowett's support whenever needed, and the two men maintained a relationship throughout their political careers. It was through Logan's favor that Rowett was named to the position of Internal Revenue Collector of the Fourth (Quincy) District by appointment of President Chester A. Arthur in 1881.** In that position, Rowett once again worked for a time with Raum, the Commissioner of Internal Revenue in Washington from 1876-83.

For much of his time in office, Rowett lived in Quincy, first at the Tremont House before taking up residence at the southeast corner of Locust and 24th. His position enabled him to recommend friends and associates for political jobs around the state, including Joseph, who joined him in Quincy and received work as a storekeeper in the same building as his brother's office. That promise landed Rowett in trouble with his old army superior,

A.J. Babcock, who was angered when Rowett could not deliver on a promise of a job for his son, creating an embarrassing predicament. That aside, Rowett capably performed in the office until 1885, when the Democratic adminstration of Grover Cleveland consolidated the district with another and appointed a member of that party to the position.

The ragged party definitions of the 1870s were far behind him, and the General had earned a place as not only a top Republican, but as a leading figure of Illinois politics. His renewed devotion to his party was evident when, following Logan's death, Rowett spoke against continuing the past divisions of Republicans that he himself had subscribed to a decade earlier.

If he accomplished nothing else in his life, Rowett's political record could stand alone as his mark in the world. In truth, few remember him for his two decades of public service and point to other, more familiar achievements.

*An obituary of Rowett reports that, in his life, "he never lost an opportunity to do a friendly act for Grant" and was "always consulted when his political interests were at stake in Illinois." In addition, Rowett served under Grant in the war and was one of the "306" who voted for him at the 1880 Republican national convention. Although he was obviously dissatisfied with the Republicans, whether Rowett was actually unhappy with the Grant administration itself is unclear.

**Some sources report that Rowett was appointed by President Garfield, rather than Arthur.

VIII
The Meadows

Before the war, Richard and Joseph had hoped to one day have their own stock farm, complete with thoroughbred horses and Jersey cattle, and they started saving money towards this dream. Through the war, they continued putting aside some of their officers' pay, which was fairly substantial; Richard earned at least $212 per month as a colonel, while Joe was bringing in $105.50 monthly as a first lieutenant when he was mustered out.

When the brothers returned home, they had accumulated enough money to buy a farm one mile north of Carlinville. They acquired some ordinary mares, which they replaced as they could with better stock. Charley, himself a hero of the war, took up residence as a top member of the stable and became a prized race horse in local runs. The Rowett stock also won countless ribbons at the annual Macoupin County Fair and continued to do so for decades.

But it was not long before the Rowetts built their farm into a breeding ground of national repute. Thoroughbreds of the highest quality with pedigrees to match were soon coming out of the farm, which the brothers named "The Meadows."

These horses proved their worth on western and southern racetracks, including frequent appearances at races in Chicago, and the Rowett colors of orange jacket and blue cap became familiar to turfmen everywhere. The Rowett horses were fairly easy to spot; in unique fashion, the General often named his thoroughbreds after family members, and the fine performances of Ella Rowett, Jennie Rowett, and Madam Rowett were long remembered by fellow horsemen.*

Breeding often kept the General on the road, taking his horses to shows and fairs across the state, including many trips to Washington Park in Chicago, a top track and trading center. His business also took him to races and shows at Saratoga, in Kentucky, and elsewhere. It proved profitable, for Rowett horses usually realized great prices at auction.

The horse trades were not always known for their integrity and character, a fact that Rowett loathed. His outspoken honesty and hatred of crookedness in thoroughbred circles lifted him above other traders and earned the respect of all who dealt with him. Rather than sell inferior stock to unwitting buyers, he would point out spots and blemishes on the horses that would have otherwise gone unnoticed. So sensitive that he could not bear criticism, the General once said that "he would sooner cut off his right hand than do any man a wrong," and, as a result, won the overwhelming respect of his peers.

Achieving such recognition in breeding was neither an easy task nor a small one. It took much effort and dedication to build The Meadows into the nationally known breeding ground that it became.

The Meadows was an impressive operation, to say the least. Situated on a tiny branch of water called Hurricane Creek, the 200-acre farm was centered around the large sheds that housed the valuable stock. Long rows of box stalls lined these "L" shaped buildings, which were replaced in the 1880s by an enormous barn constructed at a cost of $2,000, a great price at the time.

R. ROWETT.

Breeder and importer of

THOROUGHBRED AND CLYDESDALE HORSES,

Jersey Cattle.

(American Jersey Cattle Club Herd Register.)

———

"The Meadows."

A sample of the letterhead used by Rowett in his business at The Meadows.

This barn, thought to be the largest in the county, became a well-known feature of The Meadows. Inside, the horses and cattle were tended to, and exercising and training the thoroughbreds was an important part of the routine. Rowett leased an additional 40-acre tract adjacent to the east as additional pasture for brood mares and colts.

Farming the land itself was also a priority, for the General had a strong liking for that work. The farm was a large one, and since Rowett was often away from home, he employed a crew of men, headed by George Nagle, to help run this grandiose spread of breeding and agriculture. Joe continued his active role in The Meadows until 1885, when he left Carlinville for other business opportunities in Chicago.

The Meadows was not the only farm that Rowett worked. He operated a farm in Quincy while there during his term as collector. For various reasons, the General also owned land near the central Minnesota town of Willmar and, in a less rural setting, for a time owned a parcel of land within the city limits of northeastern Carlinville.

****

In 1885, a dark brown horse named Hyder Ali, a leading sire and the pride of Rowett's stock, was standing at The Meadows when the General bred him to one of his top mares, Interpose. This pairing had produced favorable offspring in past years, including Grey Cloud, a colt owned by Noah Armstrong of the Doncaster Ranch in the Northwest Territory (in what is now Montana). Grey Cloud proved to be a fine racer and enjoyed great success both as a two- and three-year-old.

Armstrong boasted a fine stable of horses, including Lord Raglan, which finished third in the 1883 Kentucky Derby. When Rowett offered Interpose for sale later in 1885, Armstrong, familiar with the high quality of her offspring, purchased her, her unborn foal, and her suckling filly, Madelin, for $1,000.

The brood was shipped to Armstrong's ranch, one-and-a-half miles from Twin Bridges. The ranch was known for its spectacular round barn, standing three stories high and complete with an indoor track. While in Spokane Falls in Washington Territory on business, Armstrong received a telegram informing him of the birth of Interpose' foal. In honor of the city, he named the colt Spokane.

A chestnut colt of small build, Spokane showed tremendous promise as a racer and won two of five starts as a two-year-old in 1888. Knowing that Spokane had the talent for greatness, Armstrong entered him in the 1889 Kentucky Derby, set for May 9.

Listed at 10-to-1 by the oddsmakers in the eight-horse field, Spokane was not expected to beat the favored Proctor Knott, a Kentucky-bred chestnut gelding that went off at 1-to-2. However, much to the shock of the then-record crowd of 25,000 at Churchill Downs, Spokane edged Proctor Knott by a nose in a thrilling finish to capture the 15th Kentucky Derby.

In doing so, Spokane set a record of 2:34 ½ over the one-and-a half mile track. The distance was shortened to its present one-and-a-fourth miles in 1896. He remains the only horse from Montana to ever win a Kentucky Derby. Many thought Spokane's victory over the highly rated Proctor Knott was a fluke, but the little chestnut colt proved himself again by beating the Kentucky favorite five days later at the Clark Stakes in Louisville.

By now, Spokane had attracted national attention, but his best was yet to come. He was entered in the American Derby on June 22 in Chicago and listed as a 6-to-5 favorite. The American Derby, one of the most prestigious races of the nineteenth century, promised to be yet another duel between Spokane and Proctor Knott, a 2-to-1 choice.

In front of a crowd estimated at anywhere from 50,000 to 75,000 at Washington Park, Spokane won by a length to become the first horse to win the Kentucky and American Derbys. His American Derby win earned him even more celebrity and set off an effort by some Illinoisans to claim Spokane as a native son--even though he was actually born in Montana.

Credible research in modern sources accurately reports that Spokane was bred in Illinois and foaled in Montana. Unfortunately, a series of historical articles on Carlinville published regionally in 1966 claim that Rowett actually raised Spokane on his farm. This is untrue; Spokane was only bred at The Meadows. Interpose was still in foal with him when she was sold, and Rowett never saw the colt either at birth or in his early days. In addition, Spokane's victories in the Kentucky and American Derbys in 1889 were two years after the General's death in 1887.

The 1966 articles also claim that Rowett at one time cared for the great pacer, Dan Patch. This, too, is false, as Dan Patch was born in 1896, nine years after Rowett's death.

Twentieth-century writers and researchers of the Kentucky Derby credit The Meadows as the site of Spokane's breeding and Montana as the place of his birth. These historians have ensured Rowett's place in turf history in connection to a Kentucky Derby champion. Of all the fine thoroughbreds bred or cared for at The Meadows, Spokane stands as the greatest of them all. It is all too sad that Rowett did not live to see those triumphs.

*Other horses in the Rowett stable at one time or another included Mary Rowett, Charley Rowett, Joe Rowett, General Rowett, Rebecca Rowett, and Edith Rowett. Additional thoroughbreds sired at The Meadows that either gained fame on racetracks or as sires or dams include Cavan, Conkling, Farrell, Hazel Kirk, Helianthus, Hermitage, Juliet, Lady of the Lake, Queen Bess, and Waddell Bryant.

IX
Beagles

As his thoroughbred trade grew, Rowett became interested in an area that was previously untapped and obscure--beagling. These little hounds were common in his native England, but beagles of true blood were not found in the United States. He imported high-quality beagles from several of the top English packs, and soon the Rowett beagles were recognized as the best of their kind. The General did not know it at the time, but his attention to beagling is the starting point of the story of one of America's best-loved dogs.

Historians of beagling credit Rowett as the first to introduce the beagles that we know today to this country. His name is found in nearly every source on beagling published in this century, and most of those volumes also note his other contributions as a pioneer of American beagling.

While writers uniformly agree that Rowett introduced the beagle to America, exactly when he did is of considerable debate. It is surprising to the modern researcher that there is such wide discrepancy in the approximate dates of the importation of the dogs. Depending on the source, intervals anywhere from the 1850s to the 1870s are given, with some works listing in general terms either the early 1800s, or, simply, sometime during the nineteenth century.

Few historians attempt to provide a certain year on this question. Eugene Lentilhon's leading 1921 book quotes a letter from a top historian of beagling that says the dogs were introduced about 1875. More recently, the 1990 publication of Musladin, Musladin, and Lueke narrows the year even further to 1876. This is likely the actual date, albeit approximate, of when the General imported the dogs. In fact, a majority of beagling sources do list the 1870s as the general period in which the dogs were introduced. Moreover, recollections written in the next century by Joe's future wife that mention the beagles give no indication that Rowett had the dogs before the war.

It should be noted that, prior to Rowett's importation, dogs known as beagles were found in America. Small hounds, some of which were called beagles, were used especially in the South for fox and hare hunting even before the Civil War. However, these dogs ("so-called beagles" in the words of one author) scarcely resembled the beagles of today, often looking more like straight-legged dachshunds or even basset hounds; and, it has been written, actually having only a slight resemblance to those two breeds. Another difference was the mostly white coat of the dogs, which had only a few dark markings.

Rowett is given credit as the first to introduce true-bred beagles to this country. One of his first dogs, Dolly, was shipped to America by his brother-in-law, and soon dogs named Rosey and Sam* were in his possession as well. It has been written that the dogs came from the northern part of England. The size, color, and physical conformity of these earliest beagles are seen in the dogs of today.

The Rowett beagles soon became the last word in beagle breeding, for their bench show form was unequalled, as was their field ability. He carefully selected his first dogs with an eye toward future breeding, and they were of the best blood with uniformity of type and even markings of white, black, and tan. Even now, beaglers are proud to find an ancestor of the Rowett strain in the pedigree of their hounds.

Although Rowett did not scatter this strain widely, some of his friends and acquaitances acquired specimens, and eventually the Rowett beagles were the recognized ones. As others took an interest in beagling, disputes over type and individual dogs arose, and by the early 1880s, there emerged a need for a beagle standard.

It led to the formation of the American-English Beagle Club, founded in 1884 by beaglers in the Philadelphia area. A committee was named to draft the first-ever beagle standard, and the task was given to Rowett, Norman Elmore of Granby, Conn., another early breeder, and Dr. L.H. Twadell of Philadelphia.

The standard was molded on the Rowett beagles, generally accepted as the finest of their time. A point scale was assigned to grade each part of a beagle, including head, neck, shoulders, chest, back, feet, coat, and tail. Defects and disqualifications per individual body area were also addressed. The complete standard is found in the appendix.

It is also interesting to note that Rowett was offered the presidency of the new club, but he turned it down, citing a lack of time due to his horse business. Later he wrote--not in the most humble of terms--of his interest in a lesser position, such as secretary, and that someone from the East was probably a more suitable candidate for the presidency.

While his dogs were the models for the standard, it is unlikely that Rowett actually wrote much of the document. An 1892 letter from Twadell states that, at the time of the appointment of the committee, Rowett was "very much occupied with his horse interests" and that he asked Twadell to "formulate a scale of points and submit for revision if required." Elmore agreed to this, and Twadell proceeded to write the standard, which he later presented to the others and, as he said, "no change whatever was suggested by either gentlemen." Thus was born the first standard for beagles, which in turn was adopted by the American Kennel Club, established later that year.

In 1887, a second organization, the National Beagle Club, was founded, but it was not allowed to join the American Kennel Club because the American-English Beagle Club (then simply known as the American Beagle Club) refused to sanction its admission. However, the two clubs merged in 1891 to become the National Beagle Club of America. In 1900, the beagle standard was revised to further emphasize the running gear of the dogs, but the document remained much the same, as it does today.

After Rowett's death, his stock was taken over by Pottinger Dorsey of New Market, Md. and C. Staley Doub of Frederick, Md. Under their care, such renowned descendants as Rambler, Rally, Lee, Venus, and Countess were produced as the Rowett strain held it place as the best in the field.

The merit received by the General in beagling, for the most part, did not come during his lifetime. In truth, it is likely that few realized the importance of the beagles that could be seen tied up across The Meadows. No mention of the dogs is made in Rowett's obituaries, although sales of the dogs do appear in records of his estate.

However, his contributions are noted in nearly every source on beagling published in the twentieth century. The bulk of the standard that bears his name is still used today, and the beagles that millions of Americans know and love are the result of those first importations. The chronicle of the beagle and its place in mainstream America is Rowett's greatest achievement of all.

*Some sources on beagling also credit another dog, Warrior, as being among Rowett's first importations. However, other sources list another early beagler, C.H. Turner, as having imported that dog.

X
Private Life

Although his prominence was growing by leaps and bounds, Rowett continued to lead a modest, semi-private existence in his personal life. After his divorce in 1864, he lived a single life for the next decade, raising his son (now known as Charles) and running his business with Joe at The Meadows.

Rowett re-married on February 12, 1874 to Eleanora Braley, a well-to-do young woman ten days shy of her 26th birthday. Ella, as she was known, was educated at Ipswitch Seminary in Boston and was the third of six children of Ellison Braley, a wealthy farmer who had previously operated a sawmill south of town rumored to be a stop on the Underground Railroad.

A woman of great spirit who loved farm life and kept abreast of agricultural progression, Ella proved to be a good match for her up-and-coming husband. They soon started a family, and their first child, Mary, was born on January 26, 1875.

A son died shortly after birth on July 14, 1877, but a healthy daughter, Edith Kimball, was welcomed into the household on June 24, 1878. A son, Richard, Jr., was born July 9, 1880, with another child, Archibel, arriving on October 16, 1883.

The growing family enjoyed the serenity of life at The Meadows, known as one of the best farms in the county. The Meadows featured an impressive array of outbuildings, including the huge barn, that housed the valuable thoroughbreds, Jersey cattle, and sheep. Handsome racehorses dotted the landscape, and beagles, then not recognized as anything special to most people, were tied up across the farm.

Ella loved to have the friends of her children come and visit the farm, and Saturdays were known as big days at the Rowett place for local youngsters, who spent hours playing and helping out with chores. A boyhood friend of Richard, Jr. wrote many years later that one task was exercising the beagle hounds, which likely was more fun than work. Young people enjoyed visiting the farm, but it must have been a unique experience for anyone who stopped in or was just passing by.

Seeing the General ride into town probably was quite a sight as well. Described as a handsome man, his strong presence, combined with the visible effects of his war wounds, would have commanded respect among the locals. A member of the local post of the Grand Army of the Republic, Rowett attended the Presbyterian Church with his family, although he belonged to no religious denomination.

However, Rowett was actually away from Carlinville and The Meadows quite often, as his breeding business kept him away from home for extended periods. Politics took him away, too, as he spent much of his term in the legislature in Springfield. He also lived the better part of three years in Quincy while internal revenue collector, although Ella and the children joined him there for at least part of his term.

But his devotion to home was unwavering, and one may infer that the time Rowett did spend at home was pleasant and satisfying. His marriage was solid, and Ella's interest in farming and support of her husband's endeavors augmented their bond. The children, all well-liked, were beginning to display the traits that would make them successful as adults. His status as a leading citizen of Carlinville also made for happiness at home, so Rowett was seemingly well set in his limited time at The Meadows.

XI
The Legend of Bay Charley

Throughout his life, Rowett travelled the country on business with breeding and had in his possession some of the finest thoroughbreds in the nation. But his old war horse, Charley, was always close to his heart.

Upon returning from the war, Charley became well-known in the Carlinville area and won the General quite a bit of money in local races. The old thoroughbred lived an honored life at The Meadows until his death in 1886, when the legend grew out of events that many would find eccentric.

As daughter Edith wrote many years later, Rowett looked out a window one morning and saw Charley on his feet on a hill east of the house, in the pasture that Rowett leased. However, after breakfast, Rowett again looked out the window and saw Charley down. The old horse's life had come to a sudden end, and Rowett later said that Charley "was game to the last" and "died on his feet."

Rowett's fondness for Charley led him and Joseph to grieve for Charley as they would for a member of the family. Both men preserved a wisp of Charley's mane as a remembrance.

Their grief also led to ceremony to honor Charley's passing, as the horse was buried in the front yard of the Rowett home in a military style funeral. A flag was placed over the grave and a military salute was fired as Charley was buried, in Edith's words, "as any other soldier."

Charley's head originally faced north in his grave, but Richard and Joe, staying true to the honor of the late war, concluded that it would be more proper that Charley should "face the enemy." As a result, they took the horse out of the grave and turned Charley around, so his head faced southward--thereby "facing the enemy."

Edith went on to say that Charley's grave was tended by surviving members of the Rowett family for years, until Ella "finally awakened to the folly of so much sentimentality and the grave was leveled off." But the story does not stop there.

Not long after Rowett's death, a local high school student named Ruth Kimball was looking for a theme for a composition class, and Ella's sister, Mrs. Catherine Keune, told the girl of the story of Bay Charley. Ruth used the story to write a poem on the horse, which added to the legend of Bay Charley.

The sprawling poem was published in the *St. Paul Globe* as well as the *Macoupin County Enquirer* at the time. A few years later, C.H.C. Anderson, a boyhood pal of Richard, Jr., won a declamation contest at Blackburn College with the poem.

In 1929, Mrs. Keune left a copy of the poem at the office of the *Carlinville Democrat*, with the request that the rhyme be sent on to her niece, Edith, in Portland, Oregon. The poem was forwarded to Edith, who in turn made a copy for publication in the paper and added some background on how the poem was created.

The poem was published in the July 3, 1929 edition of the *Democrat* as the legend of Bay Charley lived on over four decades after Rowett's death. Even today, a few area residents can still recite the story of how Rowett held a military funeral for his horse.

BAY CHARLEY
written by Ruth Kimball

Yes, Bay Charley's old and broken, stumbles when you let him run,
Growing blind, you see, and feeble--years of usefulness all done.
Still he stands there in the stable groomed and tended like a king,
Like a grand old royal fellow--has the best of everything.
Stands so still I know he's thinking of the days when yet a boy,
Charlie bore the gallant colonel of the Seventh Illinois.

You knew Rowett? Bet you knew him when his hair was streaked with
white
And he limped with rebel bullets (Shot at Allatoona's fight).
Private, colonel, and then general. Honors followed one by one*
Richard Rowett, of Macoupin, honors by his valor won.
Nature meant for him a soldier--handsome, gallant, daring, quick,
And his troopers who adored him, nicknamed him "Daredevil Dick."

May, and morning, down in Georgia, bright after a night of showers,
And a mockingbird was singing love songs to magnolia flowers.
Roses pink and white and crimson filled the air with perfume sweet,
Nodding over gates and hedges at the passers in the street.
Passers? Here and there a soldier stalked on sentry, up and down,
But the streets were blank and empty; Union soldiers held the town.

"All is quiet" down at Macon, but above the vine-hung door
Where the Stars and Bars had floated, stream the Stars and Stripes
once more.
Headquarters of brigade commander; Rowett's general in command.
At the gate he stood that morning, Charley's bridle in his hand,
For the morning was so lovely, he and Charley'd go alone
To meet the reconnoitering party, tardy in its coming home.
Out since midnight was the party, and the General at the gate,
Spurred and booted, fumed, impatient, wondering what could make
them late.
So he vaulted to his saddle, touched his hat and rode away,
Bowing to his scornful hostess, widowed for the rebel gray.
One son off with Johnston's army, gone to dare his father's fate,
And she hated Northern soldiers, with a Southern woman's hate.

But the General rode off, whistling, heart as light as Charley's feet,
Out into the open country, from the shady village street.
Briar roses in the angles of rail fences, nodded gay
Morning greetings to the soldier on the country road that day.
Soft the wind blew off the meadows, sighed among the languid trees,
And the rider bared his forehead to the scented, Southern breeze.
Now an old gate spans the highway, leaping lightly to the ground,
He turns it on his rusty hinges, passes through and swings it 'round.

At his right across the meadow, as he rides along again,
Dim and hazy in the distance, now he sees a group of men.
It's the reconnoitering party, though he cannot see a face,
There's the Union blue to prove it, so he checks Bay Charley's pace.
Turns his horse to ride and meet them, when, beneath a suit of blue,
He sees a traitor Illinoisan, a deserter whom he knew.
Union colors wear the riders, but they are all rebel men;
Quick the General checks Bay Charlie, tightened rein to turn, and then
He sees the traitor looking toward him, sees him start and hears him call:
"Catch him boys! There goes Dick Rowett, biggest devil of them all!
'Head him off!" He turns Bay Charley, "Head him off down at the gate."
And he knows the trap has caught him--knows it when it is too late.

Spurs on Charley's flank of satin, jockey's hand on Charley's reins,
And the old Kentucky bluegrass throbs to life in Charley's veins.
"Go!" the racehorse hears the order, "Go!" gives magic to his feet,
Death itself could scarcely catch him; young Bay Charley'll win the heat.
"Halt! Surrender!" On he dashes, rebel prisons flash to mind.
What? Surrender to such jailors? Better death, a thousand times!
On he dashes, rebels gaining, and a sudden burst of cheers,
(Charley thinks he's on the racetrack, and it is applause he hears.)
Thoroughbred from old Kentucky. Running! Going like the wind!
Ping! A spiteful little bullet bites the yellow dust behind.
Nearer looms the gate before him, nearer still the rebels come;
Every shout makes Charley wilder, neck and neck the race is run.

"Head him off! Now boys, we've got him!" And the rebel yell again
Stings through Charley's throbbing pulses like a sudden dart of pain.
Now the gate is just before him. Round him thick the bullets sing.
The general rises in his stirrups and gathers Charley for the spring.
Gate? He thinks it is a hurdle. Over like a bird he flies,
While the rebels just at arm's length pause a moment in surprise.
Then the bullets fly in earnest, but the general lying flat
To Bay Charley's royal body, in defiance swings his hat.
On beyond the gate he gallops, and he yells defiance too;
Skirmishers are coming toward him, his own men, in Union Blue.

Back the rebel lines are driven, and the May day sun goes down
On the general at his quarters, his brigade still holds the town.
Charley has his place of honor, and the trooper at his side
Proudly tells his sunburned comrades of the general's morning ride.
Thoroughbred from old Kentucky! Blood and bone that can't be beat!
Rebel bullets racing with him, still Bay Charley won the heat.

*This is the first of several historical inaccuracies in the poem, as Rowett entered the service as a captain. However, these nevertheless do not detract from the entertainment value of the poem, nor of the tremendous creativity of the writer, a girl approximately 16 years of age.

XII
"Died in His Stable"

By the year 1887, Richard Rowett had made quite a name for himself. Known statewide for his political exploits, he was nationally recognized in both breeding and beagling, and he enjoyed a growing family and status as one of Carlinville's leading citizens. While his financial matters were in disarray--many of his assets were highly leveraged--all seemed well in the old war hero's life.

Still active in the breeding trade, the General left for Lexington, Ky. in late April to attend a meeting. Several days later, he received a telegram from home containing sorrowful news; his youngest child, Archibel, had died on May 6.

The cause of the child's death was given as "brain trouble." Described in the Rowett family Bible as "the pet and pride of the household," the sad news of the loss of Archibel deeply shook the General.

It was later written that Rowett would see his own health begin to decline upon hearing of Archibel's death. Either due to the shock of the news or because of natural progression, Rowett began to suffer from heart disease, which would inhibit him for the remainder of his life. He suffered several spells of illness at The Meadows following his return a few weeks later.

Heart troubles were yet another health concern for the 56-year-old General, who had been diagnosed with rheumatism during the winter of 1886-87 and still battled the permanent effects of his Allatoona wounds. Due in large part to his ailing heart, Rowett was "unable to go any great distance" or engage in conversation in which he might become emotional or excited.

His busy schedule continued, though, as Rowett was the keynote speaker at a Memorial Day celebration in Carrollton. A few days later he left for Chicago on an extended trip with some of his finest colts, which he planned to sell at auction at Washington Park. While there, he also planned to attend a memorial

Survivors of the Seventh Illinois Volunteer Infantry at their first reunion in Springfield, Feb. 16, 1884, the 22nd anniversary of the fall of Fort Donelson. Of the two men standing in front of the group, Rowett is at right, hat in hand. (Reprinted from *Proceedings of the Reunion of the Association of the Survivors of the Seventh Regiment Illinois Infantry Volunteers*; photo processing by Daugherty Photography, Carlinville, Illinois)

presentation to the widow of the late John A. Logan, his longtime friend and political ally.

Shortly after the General's departure, the Rowett household suffered another troubling event as a severe storm produced a tornado that touched down on the edge of The Meadows, threatening the valuable Rowett stock. Although apparently nothing was lost, it was yet another in a long line of problems for the Rowetts as the traumatic spring of 1887 gave way to summer.

Things would not prove any easier in Chicago. On June 30, a reporter met Rowett at Washington Park after the General had just walked from the stand across the track. Rowett was about to recross the track, but expressed doubt to the reporter as to whether he could without stopping to rest, adding gravely that "unless he got some relief, he could not last much longer." A few days later, shortly after coming down from the offices of the Washington Park Club, Rowett was met by a *Chicago Tribune* reporter who said the General "was much distressed from the exertion of going up and down the stairs."

A bizarre episode on Saturday, July 9 led to further concern of Rowett's health. The General was about to get off a cable car when he realized that he had left his old field glasses, a prized possession, in his seat. He made an unsuccessful--and, in light of his condition, dangerous--attempt to jump back on the car to retrieve his glasses before a conductor, who saw the General following the car and, upon noticing the glasses still on the seat, returned them.

Rowett later acknowledged that the attempt to jump on the car nearly killed him, but he hated to lose his field glasses, which had been through the war with him. Through the glasses, he had seen sights that thrilled him as well as sights that had terrified him, and he made the effort to retrieve them, albeit aware of the danger to his health.

On Monday, July 11, Rowett's stock, fourteen colts between the ages of one and two, arrived in preparation of the sale two days later. During the day, Rowett again complained of his health to two men in the Washington Park grandstand, showing them a small vial of digitalis that he described as "almost as much as his life was worth to take, but that he had to do it."

His condition would improve, at least temporarily, that evening while attending the memorial presentation to Mrs. Logan, made by the Chicago Union Veterans Club in an ornate ceremony. He was joined at the presentation by his friend Charles T. Strattan, a former state representative from Mt. Vernon and a candidate for state superintendent of public instruction in 1882, who said that the General appeared to be in excellent health. Indeed, Strattan went riding with Rowett the following day and noted that the General was in "unusually good spirits."

****

Rowett arrived at Washington Park Wednesday morning, the thirteenth of July, to find one of his colts dead, which agitated him. He left the stables and walked across the field to watch the horses working on the inside track and did not return until around 11:30 a.m.

When he returned, he was met by a grocer who presented him with a bill of $24 for supplies furnished for the stable hands. The groceries had been purchased by a boy acting under Rowett's order, and the youngster, who had been discharged earlier in the week, swore that everything had been paid up to that time. The General demanded an itemized bill from the grocer, who was unable to produce such a document but maintained that the amount was due. Rowett believed he was being taken for the money, and an argument ensued.

The debate caused both men to question the other's honesty, and the General, with his temper and his pride, would not tolerate such insult. He raised his arm to strike the man, but his arm dropped and he staggered backwards. He called out for his stable hands to catch him, but before any could, he fell heavily against a box stall.

The stable hands carried Rowett out of the stall and attempted to revive him as best they could. His face now dark purple in color, he was stripped and rubbed with camphor, but it was too late. After one or two long gasps for breath, Rowett faded from life.

Physicians that had been sent for arrived to find the General dead, and Joseph reached his brother's side too late as well. Heart disease was given as the official cause of death, although an obituary stated that the lingering effects of his wounds from Allatoona may have been at least partially responsible.

Word of Rowett's sudden death spread quickly. Joe sent Ella a telegram informing of her husband's passing, and the new widow was stricken down upon reading the sad letter. Joe escorted the remains home to Carlinville on a late evening train.

Others soon learned of the news, which ran July 14 on page one of the *Illinois State Journal* in Springfield as well as the *Chicago Tribune* and the *Quincy Daily Journal*. The *New York Times* also carried the story as front-page news that day under the headline "Died in His Stable."

In Springfield, Palmer received the first private dispatch of Rowett's death and left for Carlinville early Thursday to assist in funeral arrangements. A special train was also run from the capital city to Carlinville to carry some of Rowett's many friends to the service, scheduled for 3 p.m. Friday, July 15.

Carlinville itself was thrown into a state of mourning, and flags were draped over buildings and city streets. The funeral was held in the Methodist Episcopal Church and drew the highest number of mourners ever for a local service.

The elaborate ceremony began with an escort of the deceased from The Meadows to the church, accompanied by the local Grand Army of the Republic post, the Gillespie Coronet Band, and visiting friends and comrades. Rowett's military record of sixty-two battles and skirmishes was read and honored before a prayer, which preceded a brief talk from Palmer, who was overcome with emotion during his address and could barely speak.

A flag from the women of the G.A.R. was pinned on the General's breast as the remains were viewed by a long line of mourners. And, in a tribute to the hero of Allatoona, the church choir serenaded the visitation with "Hold the Fort."

The Rowett family burial plot, located on the southeastern edge of Carlinville City Cemetery. The graves of Ella, Richard, Joseph, and Archibel Rowett are in the front row of the plot. The graves of Mary Rowett and her husband, William Wentworth, are to the left of the family monument, with the grave of Richard, Jr. at right. (Photo by author)

XIII
Legacy

When Rowett passed away, he unfortunately did not leave a will, so everything was thrown into probate. If it was not known before, the state of his financial condition was then realized.

It was an era in which almost all transactions were done on credit, from the smallest grocery item to the longest-term asset. In that, Rowett was no different than anyone else of the late nineteenth century, but even with his personal estate of $15,000 and the farm of $14,000 in value, it became apparent that little would be left after payment of claims.

For the next three years, there were a number of sales to auction off the valuable thoroughbreds, Jersey cattle, and other stock. The colts intended for sale the day Rowett died were sold three days later and brought good prices, as did a well-attended public sale at The Meadows the following October 27. More stock was auctioned at public sale in Chicago on July 11, 1888, but the creditors were always waiting. By the time that all claims, as well as a double mortgage on The Meadows, were settled, a total of $576.83 was left to be divided between Ella and the four surviving children when the estate was finally completed in late 1890.

Ella continued to operate the farm for some time after her husband's death, while his longtime partner, Joe, established himself in the Chicago area. At the time of Richard's death, Joe was working for a business that dealt in petroleum products, but in 1889, he landed a position at the penitentiary in Joliet that his brother had once helped administer.

That same year, Joe returned to Carlinville long enough to marry Charlotte Chapman, the 26-year-old daughter of longtime family friend Fletcher Chapman, with whom he would have two children. Joe worked with the World's Fair in Chicago in 1893 and returned to the penitentiary when the Republicans regained the Governor's mansion in 1897. As the turn of the century neared, though, his health steadily declined as rheumatism and heart troubles set in. He died on June 21, 1903 at home in Joliet and is buried next to his brother in Carlinville City Cemetery.

Back in Carlinville, the Rowett children were coming of age and heading their separate ways. Charles, the oldest son, had graduated from Blackburn, married, and left home before his father's death, going first to Colorado before moving on to Lower California to manage a ranch near Ensenada Towers, Mexico. Four children were born to him, but all died young; a son, Dick, died in young adulthood, while each of a set of triplets did not survive their first year. Little is known of what became of Charles, for information on his death is not known.

Mary and Edith were also Blackburn graduates, and Mary was named postmistress to the Illinois House of Representatives in 1894. An attractive, intelligent brunette of great social skills, she afterward landed a job in Chicago and married businessman William Wentworth there in 1901. Edith, like her sister attractive and bright, followed Mary to Chicago and worked for a time there as well.

Richard, Jr. stayed in Carlinville and helped his mother with the farm, but the family had a dream of owning a ranch in wide-open spaces. Ella and the children each chipped in, and they purchased a ranch in southwestern Nebraska near Haigler in 1901.

Life on the ranch appealled to Ella, who loved nature and farm life, and Richard, who built the ranch into a large-scale farming and cattle operation. However, Mary and her husband left three years later and returned to Chicago, where they both worked for the publishing firm of William A. Wise. When the firm moved to New York City, they went with it, and Mary, a skilled businesswoman, eventually became the circulation manager for *Current Opinion* magazine before falling ill in June 1923. She died on September 20 at age 48, survived by her husband but no children. Both Mary and William are buried in the family plot in Carlinville.

Edith, too, returned to Chicago and found a job, but her dream was to see the Pacific Ocean, and she ventured to southern California before making her way to Portland, Oregon. There, she met and in 1906 married James Reeves, the son of an influential

Illinois judge. Together, they embarked on a highly profitable idea; buying homes, refurbishing and furnishing them, and selling at a gain. Edith out-lived her siblings and passed away two days after her 73rd birthday, survived by a daughter.

As her daughters left, Ella continued to enjoy her remaining years on the ranch while travelling around to visit Mary and Edith, spending time in Chicago, southern California, and Portland. While in Oregon, she became an active member of the Portland Woman's Club and kept in touch with veterans of the Seventh who were also living there. But she became ill back home in Haigler in May 1914 and could not recover.

Throughout her life, Ella laughed that she was born on Washington's birthday and married on Lincoln's birthday, and that she hoped to die on some notable day. On August 24, 1914, she told her son, "I have your smile" just before she slipped from life. She was brought back to Carlinville and laid to rest with her family.

Richard stayed in Nebraska for the rest of his life. A cheerful soul, he was known as the "man of smiles" and enjoyed friendships across the country. He died at home on February 21, 1929 and was buried in Carlinville, survived by his wife of nearly 22 years, Blanche.

****

If children are one's greatest legacy, then, based on the successes of his own, Rowett left this world in grand style. But he left behind much more, too.

On July 5, 1888, two-year-old Spokane made his racing debut in Chicago in the Hyde Park Stakes, ran at Washington Park-- the site of his breeder's death. The following May, the little colt ensured his place in American sports history with a victory in the biggest race of all, the Kentucky Derby. He then came back to Washington Park and added to his own legacy with a win at the American Derby.

As Spokane raced his way into history, the beagle was just gaining a foothold in America. Soon, beagles were known across the nation, and they went on to become one of this country's most popular dog breeds. Millions of Americans are beagle owners, and millions more laugh every morning at the adventures of another famous beagle--the cartoon variety--in the comic strip *Peanuts*.

Rowett could not have known that beagles would grow to what they have become, and he could not have known that one of the horses bred at The Meadows would earn such acclaim. But he must have known the extent of the achievements he reached in his lifetime.

His service, integrity, and eloquence gave his name a place in the annals of Illinois political history. Even more important is his military record, indomitably led by his stand at Allatoona that may well have saved Sherman's plan to march to the sea. The battle was the defining moment of Rowett's life; it is what is inscribed on his tombstone.

Richard Rowett was not a wealthy man, and, based on his temper and his mourning of Bay Charley, he was at times eccentric. But his contributions are indisputable and have actually grown with time.

On the day of Rowett's death, Senator Shelby Cullom was in Chicago and learned of the news that evening. In a printed interview, Cullom remembered Rowett as "a vigorous, active, earnest kind of man in whatever he believed. He was always considered an honorable man, a brave soldier, and a good citizen."

Rowett would have wanted to be remembered that way.

Appendix
Beagle Standard of the American-English Beagle Club

Remarks
Beagle Breeders are aware of the fact that a Standard and Scale of Points are an absolute necessity, so that an authorized type of the Beagle Hound is made apparent for Bench Show Judges to base their decisions upon, as no two are similar in opinion as to merit, and their ideas differ widely in their estimates as to quality and the breed marks of the race.

To avoid having harrier sized dogs recognized at one show and the smallest specimens favored at another, is one of the objects sought to remedy by the compilers of the Standard and Scale of Points of the American Beagle Club, as with an accepted standard the Judge will have a guide to lead him through the difficulties of his position, and the breeder if a novice will be enabled with its assistance to discard those animals that are deficient in quality, and recognize merit where it exists, thus elevating the status of the kennel.

HEAD. The skull should be moderately domed at the occiput, with the cranium broad and full. The ears set on low, long and fine in texture, the forward or front edge closely framed and in-turned to the cheek, rather broad and round at the tips, with an almost entire absence of erectile power at their origin.

The eyes full and prominent, rather wide apart, soft and lustrous brown or hazel in color. The orbital processes well developed. The expression gentle, subdued and pleading. The muzzle of medium length, squarely cut, the stop well defined. The jaws should be level, lips either free from or with moderate flews. Nostrils large, moist, open.

Defects--A flat skull, narrow across the top of the head, absence of bone. Ears short, set on too high, or when dog is excited, rising above the line of the skull at their points of origin, due to an excess of erectile power. Ears pointed at the tips, thick or boardy in substance, or carried out from cheek, showing a space between. Eyes of a light or yellow color. Muzzle long and snipy. Pig jaws or the reverse, known as undershot; lips showing deep, pendulous flews.

Disqualifications--Eyes close together, small, beady and terrier-like.

NECK AND THROAT. Neck rising free and light from shoulders, strong in substance, yet not loaded, of medium length. The throat clean and free from folds of skin; a slight wrinkle below the angle of the jaw, however, may be allowable.

Defects--A thick, short, cloddy neck, carried on a line with the top of the shoulder. Throat showing dewlap and folds of skin to a degree termed throatiness.

SHOULDERS AND CHEST. Shoulders somewhat declining, muscular but not loaded, conveying idea of freedom and action,with lightness, activity, and strength. Chest moderately broad and full.

Defects--Upright shoulders and a disproportionately wide chest.

BACK, LOINS, AND RIBS. Back short, muscular and strong; loin broad and slightly arched, and the ribs well sprung, giving abundant lung room.

Defects--A long or swayed back, a flat, narrow loin, or a flat, constricted rib.

FORELEGS AND FEET. Fore legs straight with plenty of bone, feet close, firm and either round or pear like in form.

Defects--Out elbows. Knees knuckled over or forward, or bent backward. Feet open and spreading.

HIPS, THIGHS, HIND LEGS, AND FEET. Hips strongly muscled, giving abundant propelling power. Stifles strong and well let down. Hocks firm, symmetrical and moderately bent. Feet close and firm.

Defects--Cow hocks and open feet.

TAIL. The tail should be carried gayly, well up and with medium curve, rather short as compared with the size of the dog and closed with a decided brush.

Defects--A long tail with a teapot curve.

Disqualifications--A thinly haired, rattish tail with entire absence of brush.

COAT. Moderately coarse in texture and of good length.

Disqualifications--A short, close and nappy coat.

HEIGHT. The meaning of the term "beagle," a word of Celtic origin, and in old English "Begele," is small, little. The dog was so named for its diminutive size. Your committee therefore, for the sake of consistency and that the beagle shall be in fact what his name implies, strongly recommended that the height line be sharply drawn at fifteen inches, and that all dogs exceeding that height shall be disqualified as overgrown and outside the pale of recognition.

COLOR. All hound colors are admissible. Perhaps the most popular is black, white, and tan. Next in order is the lemon and white, then blue and lemon and mottled, then follow the solid colors, such as the black and tan, tan, lemon, fawn, etc.

This arrangement is, of course, arbitrary, the question being one governed entirely by fancy.

The colors first named form the most lively contrast and blend better in the pack, the solid colors being sombre and monotonous to the eye.

It is not intended to give a point value to color in the scale for judging; as before said, all true hound colors being correct. The foregoing remarks upon the subject are therefore simply suggestive.

GENERAL APPEARANCE. A miniature foxhound, solid and big for his inches, with the wear and tear look of the dog that can last in the chase and follow his quarry to the death.

NOTE. Dogs possessing such serious faults as are enumerated

78

under the headings of disqualifications are under the grave suspicion of being of impure blood.

Under the heading of defects, objectionable features are indicated. Such departures from the standard, not however, impuging the purity of the breeding.

Scale of Points.

Summary -   Value.

Skull..5
Ears..10
Eyes..10
Muzzle, jaws, and lips.............................5
Value of head...................................35

Neck...5
Shoulders and chest...............................10
Back and loins...15
Ribs...5
Value of body...................................35

Fore legs and feet....................................10
Hips, thighs, and hind legs......................10
Value of running gear..................20

Tail...5
Coat..5
Value of coat and stern..................10
Total points.....................................100

Bibliography

PRIMARY SOURCES
Letters and Privately Held Material

Letters of Richard Rowett, 1881-85. Privately held by Rowett family descendants.

Letter of Stacy D. Allen, Shiloh National Military Park historian, to author. Dated June 28, 1992.

Letter of Theresa Fitzgerald, librarian of *Blood-Horse Magazine*, to author. Dated June 18, 1992.

Letter of Margaret G. Rogers, executive director, Northeast Mississippi Museum Association, Corinth, Miss., to author. Dated April 232, 1997.

Rowett family Bible. Privately held by Rowett family descendants.

Stoddard, Harriet. Unpublished research on Rowett and Braley families. 1974. Blackburn College library, Carlinville, Illinois.

Tansey, Charlotte (Chapman Rowett). Typed recollections. Privately held.

Government and Church Documents

Macoupin County, Illinois birth records. Macoupin County Courthouse, Carlinville, Illinois.

Macoupin County, Illinois divorce records. Macoupin County Courthouse, Carlinville, Illinois.

Macoupin County, Illinois grantee/grantor records. Macoupin County Courthouse, Carlinville, Illinois.

Macoupin County, Illinois marriage records. Macoupin County Courthouse, Carlinville, Illinois.

Macoupin County, Illinois probate records. Macoupin County Courthouse, Carlinville, Illinois.

82

Naturaliztion Certificate of Richard Rowett. Johnson County
Courthouse, Franklin, Indiana.
Records of the Anglican parish of St. Martin on Looe Bay. East
Looe, Cornwall, England.
United States Military Pension Records of Joseph Rowett.
National Archives, Library of Congress, Washington, D.C.
United States Military Service Records of Joseph Rowett.
National Archives, Library of Congress, Washington, D.C.
United States Military Service Records of Richard Rowett.
National Archives, Library of Congress, Washington, D.C.

Newspapers

Carlinville (Ill.) *Free Democrat/Carlinville Democrat*
Chicago Inter-Ocean
Chicago Tribune
Illinois State Journal
Illinois State Register
Macoupin County Argus (Carlinville, Ill.)
*Macoupin Spectator/Macoupin Enquirer/Macoupin County
    Enquirer/Macoupin Daily Enquirer* (Carlinville, Ill.)
New York Times
Oregon Journal (Portland, Ore.)
Quincy (Ill.) *Daily Journal*

SECONDARY SOURCES
Books and Articles

Ambrose, Daniel Lieb. *History of the Seventh Regiment Illinois
    Volunteer Infantry.* Springfield, Ill.: Illinois Journal
    Company, 1868.
American Stud Book. New York: Bruce, 1885.

Arnn, Barbara. *Beagles.* Kansas City: Andrews and McNeel, 1996.

Atlas of Johnson County, Indiana.

Austin, Mary Hunter. *Earth Horizon.* Cambridge, Mass.: Riverside Press, 1932.

Bailey, Robert E., and Elaine Shemoney Evans. *Descriptive Inventory of the Archives of the State of Illinois.* 2nd ed. Springfield: Office of the Secretary of State, 1997.

Boatner, Mark Mayo. *The Civil War Dictionary.* New York: The David McKay Company, 1959.

Brown, Joseph M. *The Battle of Allatoona.* Atlanta: Record Publishing Co., 1890.

Brown, W.B. *The History of a Famous Court House Located at Carlinville, Illinois.* Carlinville, Ill.: Press of the Carlinville Democrat, 1934.

Carney, Lucille. *Carlinville.* Reprint of a series of articles from the *Illinois State Journal* from June and July, 1966. Springfield, Ill.: 1966.

Clark, Reggie. "About the Dogs." *Outdoors in Illinois* Autumn 1951. p. 14.

Collier's World Atlas and Gazateer. New York: P.F. Collier and Son, 1943.

Columbo, Henry J. et al. *The New Complete Beagle.* New York: Howell Book House, 1978.

Columbus-Belmont State Park Pamphlet. Published by the Kentucky Department of Parks. 1996.

French, Samuel G. *Two Wars: An Autobiography.* Nashville: Confederate Veteran, 1901.

Hamilton, James J. *The Battle of Fort Donelson.* New York: Thomas Yoseloff, 1968.

Hesseltine, William B. *Ulysses S. Grant, Politican.* New York: Frederick Ungar Publishing Company, 1957.

Hicken, Victor. *Illinois in the Civil War.* Urbana, Ill.: University of Illinois Press, 1966.

History of Macoupin County, Illinois. Philadelphia: Brink,

MacDonough and Co., 1879.

Hochwalt, A.F. *Beagles and Beagling.* Cincinnati: Sportsman's Digest Publishing Co., 1923.

Howard, Robert P. *Mostly Good and Competent Men: Illinois Governors from 1818 to1988.* Springfield, Ill.: Illinois Issues, Sangamon State University and Illinois State Historical Library, 1988.

Hubert, Charles F. *History of the Fiftieth Illinois* Volunteer *Infantry in the War for the Union.* Kansas City, Mo.: Western Veteran Publishing Co., 1894.

Hughes, Nathaniel Cheairs, Jr. *The Battle of Belmont: Grant Strikes South.* Chapel Hill, N.C.: University of North Carolina Press, 1991.

Jones, Arthur F., and Ferelith Hamilton. *The World Encyclopedia of Dogs.* New York: World Publishing Co., 1971.

Journal of the Illinois State House of Representatives 30th General Assembly. 1877.

Korn, Jerry, and editors of Time-Life Books. *War on the Mississippi.* Alexandria, Va.: Time-Life Books, 1985.

Leach, George B. *The Kentucky Derby Diamond Jubilee.* Louisville, Ky.: Gibbs-Inman, 1949.

Lentilhon, Eugene. *Forty Years Beagling in the United States.* New York: E.P. Dutton and Co., 1921.

Lewis, Lloyd. *Sherman: Fighting Prophet.* New York: Harcourt and Brace, 1958.

Macoupin County Courthouse Centennial 1867-1967. 1967.

Malone, Dumas, ed. *Dictionary of American Biography.* vol. IX. New York: Charles Scribner's Sons, 1932.

Menke, Frank G. *The Encyclopedia of Sports.* New York: A.S. Barnes and Co., 1963.

Moses, John. *Illinois Historical and Statistical.* 2 vols. Chicago: Fergus Printing Company, 1892.

Musladin, Judith M., A.C. Musladin, and Ada Lueke. *The New Beagle.* New York: Howell Book House, 1990.

Nardinger, Susan R. *Spirit Horse of the Rockies*. Great Falls, Mt.:
   Spirit Horse Enterprises, 1988.
Neilson, James W. *Shelby M. Cullom: Prairie State Republican*.
   Urbana, Ill.: University of Illinois Press, 1962.
Nevin, David, and editors of Time-Life Books. *The Road to
   Shiloh*. Alexandria, Va.: Time-Life Books 1983.
Nevin, David, and editors of Time-Life Books. *Sherman's March*.
   Alexandria, Va.: Time-Life Books, 1986.
Nominations to Stakes and Declarations 1885-86. New York:
   D.W. Higgins and Co., 1886.
Office of the Superintendent of Public Instruction for Illinois.
   Illinois at War 1861-65. 1968.
Palmer, George Thomas. *A Conscientous Turncoat: The Story of
   John M. Palmer, 1817-1900*. New Haven, Ct.: Yale
   University Press, 1941.
Portrait and Biographical Record of Macoupin County, Illinois.
   Chicago: Biographical Publishing Co., 1891.
Prentice, Henry Wilson. *The Beagle in America and England*.
   DeKalb, Ill.: Chronicle Publishing Co., 1920.
*Proceedings of the Reunion Held in 1906 by the Association of
   Survivors Seventh Regiment Illinois Infantry Volunteers at
   Springfield, Illinois*. Springfield, Ill.: State Register
   Printing House, 1907.
Quincy, Illinois City Directory 1882-83.
Quincy, Illinois City Directory 1884-85.
Raum, Green B. *History of Illinois Republicanism*. Chicago:
   Rollins Publishing Co., 1900.
Reece, Brig. Gen. J.N. *Report of the Adjutant General of the State
   of Illinois*. vol. 1. Springfield, Ill.: Phillips Bros. State
   Printers, 1900.
Rogers, Margaret Greene. *Civil War Corinth*. Corinth, Miss.:
   Rankin Printing, 1987.
Scaife, William R. *Allatoona Pass: A Needless Effusion of Blood*.
   Etowah Valley (Ga.) Historical Society, 1995.
Scott, Berkeley. "In a Class by Himself." *The Thoroughbred*

Record 2 Mar. 1983. p. 1366.

Sherman, William Tecumseh. *Memoirs of General William T. Sherman.* Reprint. vol. 2. Bloomington, Ind.: Indiana University Press, 1957.

Smith, Theodore Clarke. *The Life and Letters of James Abram Garfield.* vol. 2. New Haven, Ct.: Yale University Press, 1925.

Sword, Wiley. *Shiloh: Bloody April.* Dayton, Ohio: Morningside Books, 1983.

Trimble, Harvey M., ed. *History of the 93rd Illinois Volunteer Infantry from Organization to Muster Out.* Chicago: Blakely Printing Co., 1898.

U.S. War Department. *The War of the Rebellion: A Compilation of the Official Records of the Union and Confederate Armies.* 128 vols. Washington: Government Printing Office, 1927.

Van Deusen, Glyndon G. *Horace Greeley: Nineteenth-Century Crusader.* Philadelphia: Univeristy of Pennsylvania Press, 1953.

Vriends-Parent, Lucia. *Beagles.* New York: Barron's, 1987.

Walker, Charles A. *History of Macoupin Co., Illinois, Biographical and Pictorial.* vol. 1. Chicago: The S.J. Clarke Publishing Co., 1911.

Whitney, George D. *This is the Beagle.* Neptune City, N.J.: TFH Publications, 1955.

Reference Notes

Opening Statement

In writing this book, I found that a substantial portion of information came from only one source; that is, a sentence of text was derived from one volume, the next sentence was derived from another volume, and so on.

Seeing this, I felt that footnotes, used with any interpretation, would be inappropriate for this text, as would endnotes. What I felt would be the best style--and the one that I eventually used--was taken from a source that provided information for this volume.

That book, *Shiloh: Bloody April*, by Wiley Sword (Morningside Books, 1983) employed much the same style that I have used. For those of you who do not understand my note system, here is a sample:

19 Rowett assumes command, Ambrose 248, Hubert 287;

The numbers in **bold** refer to the page on which the note occurs. Following is a paraphrased version of the information that is being documented; in this example, the full quote reads, "on August 15 Rowett assumed command of the Third Brigade of the Fourth Division..." The shortened version, therefore, is "Rowett assumes command," as is seen in the note.

What follows is the source and page number from which the information is derived. Here, it is from page 248 of Ambrose and page 287 of Hubert.

I also recognized that the concept of common knowledge would be a problem in my notes, for, as I said, there were many derivations of information from only one source. For that reason, much of my text--sometimes, several times in one paragraph--is individually documented.

With these thoughts in mind, I declared "common knowledge" to be information that appears in more than three sources. I remained true to this philosophy for the most part in my documentation, except in certain cases where appropriate.

The brief bibliographical essays that precede each set of notes are intended to provide additional documentation not only to my work but also for any researchers that follow who may be pursuing similar projects.

Tom Emery
August 1997

Chapter I -- Beyond Cornwall

Information on Rowett's early life is scarce, at best. Little is known of his early years in England, and details of his three years in Indiana are not found in standard sources.

The 1891 *Portrait and Biographical Record of Macoupin County* is the best source for early information on Rowett. Much of the rest comes from nontraditional sources, such as his naturalization certificate.

1 marriage of William and Jenny Rowett, church records; **1** ten children in family, Tansey 34; **1** Richard's christening, church records; **1** common school education, *Portrait and Biographical Record* 205, *Chicago Tribune* July 14, 1887; **1** wanting more from life, *Portrait and Biographical Record* 205; **1** studies history, etc., *Portrait and Biographical Record* 205; **1** well-informed and educated, *Portrait and Biographical Record* 205; **1** family members emigrate, Tansey 34; **1** boards in June at Liverpool, naturalization certificate; **2** docks on July 26, naturalization certificate; **2** population and profile of Johnson County, *Atlas of Johnson County*; **2** three years working, *Portrait and Biographical Record* 205; **2** naturalized, naturalization certificate.

Chapter II -- Carlinville

Details of Rowett's life from 1854-61 are more abundant than data on his early years, but are still hard to find. Austin describes Rowett in her work in some depth. Newspaper accounts from both that period and after Rowett's death offer more to the researcher. Tansey's recollections add to the description of Rowett's early years.

Evidence of Democratic support in Macoupin County is relatively easy to find, as both local papers refer to it repeatedly. Descriptions of Carlinville itself may be found in the Macoupin County history books of 1879, 1891, 1904, and 1911. Again, the 1891 volume is best for Rowett in terms of detail.

3 Macoupin Creek named, Moses 1138; **3** population count, *History of Macoupin County* 51; **3** Palmer activities, Howard 147, Palmer 15, 20, 24; **3** two-day journey, Palmer 10; **3** Rowett as farmer, Hicken 301; **3** works in various ways, Tansey 34; **3** works as carriage trimmer, *Chicago Inter-Ocean* July 14, 1887; **3** Joseph, Tansey 34; **3** dream of stock farm, Tansey 34; **4** Rowett and Hunter, Austin 10; **4** believes in temperance, *Carlinville Democrat* July 21, 1887, *Chicago Inter-Ocean* July 14, 1887, *Illinois State Register* July 16, 1887; **4** never indulged, *Carlinville Democrat* July 21, 1887; **4** remained true, *Carlinville Democrat* July 21, 1887; **4** ahead of his time, *Illinois State Register* July 16, 1887; **4** Lincoln loses Macoupin, *Carlinville Free Democrat* Nov. 15, 1860, Dec. 1, 1864; **5** Rowett opposes slavery, *Illinois State Register* July 16, 1887, *Carlinville Democrat* July 21, 1887; **5** Austin claims, Austin 11; **5** thrashes county official, *Chicago Tribune* July 14, 1887; **5** Rowett was first voice heard, *Illinois State Journal* July 16, 1887; **5** enlists within twenty-four hours, Austin 26; **5** helps raise company, Tansey 36; **5** "Carlinville Invincibles," *Carlinville Free Democrat* Apr. 25, 1861; **5** mustered in, *Illinois A.G. Report* 384; **5** numeric exemptions for Mexico, *Illinois A.G. Report* 384; **5** honor accorded, *Illinois A.G. Report* 384; **5-6** sent to Alton, Ambrose 7; **6** harsh quarters, Ambrose 7.

Chapter III -- Campaigns in Tennessee

Rowett's record in the war in 1861-62 often must be traced to the specific brigade or division to which the Seventh was assigned. From there, the researcher must consult individual battle sources in chronological order.

The Illinois Adjutant General's report offers a brief, yet detailed, capsule of the Seventh's activities during the war. Ambrose's day-by-day descriptions provide much more detail as well as that author's personal views.

Hughes' work on Belmont gives somewhat of an idea of what Rowett was doing through that battle. Hamilton's well-written book on Fort Donelson is very helpful, while Sword's definitive work on Shiloh makes several references to the Seventh. Information on Corinth is harder to locate, but Korn and Greene both provide a general description. Boatner's landmark work gives additional information on each battle and corresponding campaigns.

7 camped in Missouri, Ambrose 13-14; **7** *Illinois A.G. Report* 384; **7** pursue Thompson, Ambrose 14; **7** Seventh in District of Cairo, *Illinois A.G. Report 384*; **7** occupying Belmont, Hughes 4, *Columbus-Belmont Battlefield Map*; **7** southward from Fort Holt, *Illinois A.G. Report* 384, Ambrose 17-18, Hughes 56; **7** ordered back to Fort Holt, *Illinois A.G. Report* 384, Ambrose 18; **7** January expedition to Columbus, *Illinois A.G. Report* 384, Ambrose 21-23; **8** leave Fort Holt, *Illinois A.G. Report* 384, Ambrose 25; **8** reasons for taking forts, Boatner 394; **8** at rear of Henry, Ambrose 26-27; **8** Cook on left flank, Hamilton 78, 80; **8** temperatures drop, Boatner 396; **8** remained on left, battle maps in Hamilton; **8** last charge, Boatner 396, *Illinois A.G. Report* 384, Hamilton 256, 273; **8** Cook advances on east, Hamilton 273; **8** moved on extreme left, battle maps in Hamilton; **8** 14th Iowa precedes Seventh, *Illinois at* War

16; **8** Confederate losses, Boatner 397; **8** Smith credited, Boatner 769; **8** Union casualties, Boatner 397; **8** Seventh casualties and Company K, Ambrose 37-38; **8-9** Rowett praised in Ambrose, 42; **9** Rowett quote in Ambrose, Ambrose 42 **9**, Babcock ill, *Illinois A.G. Report* 384, Ambrose 43; **9** sent to Pittsburg Landing, Ambrose 44-45; **9** miserable conditions waiting to disemark, Ambrose 46-47,Sword 37; **9** purpose of Shiloh campaign, Boatner 752; **10** Seventh engaged at 8 a.m., Allen letter; **10** sent to Duncan field, Allen letter, Sword 242-243; **10** right flank of Hornet's Nest, Allen letter, Sword 281;**10** Wallace succeeds Smith, Sword 121; **10** eleven attacks, Boatner 754; **10** 62 guns, Sword 291; **10** Rowett sees Confederates, Allen letter; **10** no support and low ammunition, Sword 295; **10** Rowett led forces northeast, Sword 296, Allen letter; **10** enemy helped break Union lines, Allen letter; **10** Seventh joins McClernand, *Illinois A.G. Report* 384, Allen letter; **10** Rowett's horse shot, *Illinois A.G. Report* 384, Ambrose 52; **10** repulse of last charge, *Illinois A.G. Report* 384; **10** slept on arms, Allen letter; **10** Seventh hotly contested, Allen letter, *Illinois A.G. Report* 384; **11** Rowett twice wounded, Ambrose 63; **11** wounded in left breast, *Carlinville Free Democrat* Apr. 24, 1862; **11** Ambrose compliments Rowett, Ambrose 63; **11** sent to northern hospital, U.S. Military Records--R. Rowett; **11** to Carlinville, *Carlinville Free Democrat* May 1, 1862; **11** promoted, Boatner 711, U.S. Military Records--R. Rowett; **11** marriage in 1862, Tansey 37; **11** participated in advance, Ambrose 66-68, *Illinois A.G. Report* 385; **11** Babcock assumes command, Ambrose 82; **11** colors replaced, Ambrose 82; **11** result of Corinth abandonment, Nevin, *Shiloh*, 101; **11**, goal of recapturing Corinth, Korn 37; **12** waited out attack, Ambrose 86-89; **12** Rosecrans unprepared, Boatner 177, Korn 40; **12** weight of attack, Korn 40; **12** water in want, *W of R* I-29-1-293; **12** unseasonable heat, Korn 40; **12** intensity against center, Korn 40, Rogers 33; **12** Union regiments broke, joined by others, *W of R* I-29-1-291; **12** Rowett rallies Seventh against rear fire, *W of R* I-29-1-291; **12** rear fire renews as battery opens gun, *Wof R* I-29-1-291, Rogers letter; **12** Seventh holds, *W of R* I-29-1-291, 292, 293; **12**

92
battle losses, Korn 44; **12** Rowett wounded, *Portrait and Biographical Record* 205; **12** praised by superiors, *W of R* I-29-1-292, 294.

Chapter IV -- Valiant Officer

Ambrose's greatest gifts are his anecdotes and detailed descriptions of day-to-day life on the front. This chapter includes some of those stories.

As before, the Illinois Adjutant General's report offers a concise sketch of the Seventh's activities through the war. Hicken gives background on the problems of re-enlistment, and he, Ambrose, the Adjutant General, and period newspapers all mention to varying degrees the reception of the Seventh while on furlough in Springfield.

The Copperhead influence is stressed in Palmer and, again, is demonstrated over and over in local newspaper accounts.

13 garrison and scouting, *Illinois A.G. Report* 385, Ambrose 123-130; **13** "confiscation and extermination," Ambrose 130; **13** cut off on half rations, Ambrose 128; **13** mail did not come, Ambrose 129-132; **13** birth date of son, Rowett family Bible; **13** name of son, Macoupin County divorce records; **13-14** episode in sweet potato patch, Ambrose 110-111; **14** ordered into northern Alabama, *Illinois A.G. Report* 385, Ambrose 146-147; **14** several days spent, *Illinois A.G. Report* 385, Ambrose 147-155; **14** Rowett commander, U.S. Military Records-R.Rowett, *Illinois A.G.Report* 385; **14** Roddey, Boatner 706; **14** episode crossing river, Ambrose 157-158; **14** garrrison duty, *Illinois A.G.Report* 385, Ambrose 159, 170-171; **14** mounted, *Illinois A.G. Report* 385, Ambrose 173-174; **14-15** stories of breaking mules, Ambrose 174; **15** more rein to Charley, Ambrose 173; **15** Rowett finds Charley, *Carlinville Democrat* July 3, 1929; **15** Charley walks single plank, *Carlinville Democrat* July 3, 1929; **15** Rowett reconnoiters, jumps Charley, *Carlinville Democrat* July 3, 1929; **15** surround plantation near Purdy, Ambrose 175; **15** set up

Chapter V -- Allatoona

The Battle of Allatoona is covered in general detail in both Boatner and Nevin. Many other authoritative Civil War sources also mention the battle, often in passing.

Two works dedicated solely to the battle, Brown (1890) and Scaife's definitive 1995 publication, contribute strongly to the historical record of Allatoona. Regimental histories provide precise background as well, although such books are obscure and rare. Hubert (50th Illinois) and Trimble (93rd Illinois) both describe the battle in varying degrees, with Trimble by far the more thorough of the two. Ambrose's work gives little relevant detail, although his compliments of Rowett and others are always worthwhile reading.

Sherman's memoirs contain a brief, yet detailed, sketch of the battle, while French attempts to "set the record straight" as he sees it with his own recollections, some of which dispute popular perception of the battle.

21 Forrest's raiding, Boatner 306, Nevin, *Sherman,* 19; **21** Hood tears up railroads, Nevin, *Sherman*, 20; **21** depot and supplies, Nevin, *Sherman*, 20, Boatner 8; **22** Federal advance, Nevin, *Sherman*, 20; **22** Corse's reputation, Nevin, *Sherman*, 20; **22** Rowett's strength, Sherman 148, Hubert 295; **22** rounds of ammunition, Scaife 13; **22** men sent by rail, Nevin, *Sherman*, 20, Sherman 148, Scaife 13; **22** train derails, Hubert 295, Scaife 13, Nevin, *Sherman,* 21; **22** descriptions of Allatoona, Trimble 102-108, Brown 3-4; **22** men slept on arms, Scaife 22; **22** French's night march, Boatner 8; **23** Sears' attack on communications, Boatner 8, Nevin, *Sherman*, 21; **23** French does not receive reply, Scaife 24, Brown 6-7, French 258; **23** Cockrell attacks, joined by Young, Scaife 26; **23** Seventh buys Henry rifles, *Illinois A.G. Report* 387; **23** Rowett about to be overrun, Scaife 28; **23** Tourtelotte's fire from east, Hubert 299, Scaife 28; **25** Rowett's wound, Ambrose 255, U.S. Military Records--R. Rowett; **25** Sherman's exclamation of Corse's arrival, Nevin, *Sherman*, 24; **25** journalists' translations, Nevin, *Sherman,* 27, Boatner 8; **25** Rowett receives dispatch, *Chicago Tribune* July 14, 1887, *Illinois State Journal* July 14, 1887; **26** rebels behind stumps and logs, Brown 12, Nevin, *Sherman*, 26; **26** ammunition running low, Nevin, *Sherman,* 26; **26** barrels too hot to touch, Scaife 26; **26** Rowett conserves ammunition, Nevin, *Sherman*, 26, Lewis 428; **26** Rowett felled by

Chapter VI -- Returning War Hero

Rowett's early political career is described in the *Carlinville Free Democrat*, particularly in his campaign for county clerk. Background on the courthouse controversy is covered in unbiased fashion in both the *Macoupin County Courthouse Centennial 1867-1967* as well as in Brown. Walker, one of the outspoken opponents of the courthouse, recaps the controversy in, of course, a more slanted manner. The 1879 Macoupin County history book also devotes considerable space to the history of the courthouse.

96

33 Carlinville plans town meeting, *Carlinville Free Democrat* Aug. 17, 1865, Aug. 24, 1865; **33** Rowett appointed marshal, *Carlinville Free Democrat* Aug. 17, 1865; **33** march is lighthearted stroll, *Carlinville Free Democrat* Aug. 24, 1865; **33** Carlinville turns out, *Carlinville Free Democrat*, Aug. 24, 1865; **33** Union County Convention, *Carlinville Free Democrat* Aug. 24, 1865; **34** stars questioned, *Carlinville Free Democrat* Aug. 31, 1865; **34** Democrat blasts in turn, *Carlinville Free Democrat* Aug. 31, 1865; **34** Rowett debates Flynn, *Carlinville Free Democrat* Oct. 19. 1865; **34** Democrat mocks Flynn, *Carlinville Free Democrat* Oct. 19, 1865; **34** Rowett embarrasses and exposes Flynn, *Carlinville Free Democrat* Oct. 19, 1865; **34-35** Holliday, *Courthouse Centennial* 35, Brown 13; **35** met in public appearances, *Carlinville Free Democrat* Oct. 19, 1865; **35** Rowett "whoops 'em up," Tansey 42-43; **35** election results, *Carlinville Free Democrat* Nov. 16, 1865; **35** Charley at the races, *Carlinville Free Democrat* Nov. 23, 1865; **35** issues raised in 1865 elections, *Courthouse Centennial* 6; **35** fears of county division, *Courthouse Centennial* 11, Brown 2; **35** need new, larger building, *Courthouse Centennial* 11, Walker 162; **36** annexed to Sangamon, *Courthouse Centennial* 11; **36** make Carlinville capital, *Courthouse Centennial* 11; **36** cost in Janaury 1869, Brown 5; **36** Loomis with absolute power, *Courthouse Centennial* 13, Brown 4; **36** DuBois' firm, *Courthouse Centennial* 13, *History of Macoupin County 1879* 44; **36** 1865 population, Brown 34; **36** "taxation without representation," *Courthouse Centennial* 15; **36** confiscatory taxes and duplicated numbers, Walker 164, *Courthouse Centennial* 19; **36** Rowett speaks against legislation, *Carlinville Democrat* Feb. 25, 1869, *Courthouse Centennial* 19; **37** names of citizens on committee, *Carlinville Democrat* Feb. 25, 1869, *Courthouse Centennial* 19; **37** armed with petitions, *Courthouse Centennial* 19; **37** no limit on cost, Walker 160, 164-165; **37** citizens recognized, *Courthouse Centennial* 19; **37** costs blown up, Walker 164-165, *Courthouse Centennial* 16; **37** township government, *Courthouse Centennial* 21; **37** Holliday indicted, Brown 13; **37** fifteen separate indictments, Walker 166; **37**

advocate of common man, *Illinois State Register* July 16, 1887, *Carlinville Democrat* July 21, 1887.

Chapter VII -- Political Aspirations

Information on Rowett's political career is more abundant and easier to find that on any other aspect of his life. The Carlinville newspapers cover the 1876 election in detail and also make mention of his other political highlights.

Moses' landmark work refers to Rowett on several occasions and gives much background to the issues that involve Rowett, such as the debates of the 1880 conventions. Raum and Neilson provide additional background, as do Hesseltine and Smith, although neither specifically mention Rowett.

Rowett's defection to the Liberal Republicans is brought up in Moses and in his obituaries. Palmer's thorough 1941 study discusses the Liberal Republican movement very well, as it does with 19th-century Illinois politics as a whole. Howard does much the same in his work, while Van Deusen's biography of Greeley adds more information on the Liberal Republicans.

The Chicago newspapers write of Rowett's political achievements at various times, while the *Illinois State Journal* gives an in-depth account of the 1874 convention of the Illinois State Reform Party. Palmer and Moses also are worth consultation on that issue.

39 aligned on slavery issue, *Illinois State Register* July 16, 1887, *Carlinville Democrat* July 21, 1887; **39** Palmer supports courthouse, *Courthouse Centennial* 19, Brown 14-15, Walker 165; **39** lasting friendship, *Carlinville Democrat* July 21, 1887, *Illinois State Register* July 16, 1887, *Macoupin County Enquirer* Nov. 23, 1876; **39** appointed canal trustee, Moses I-467; **39** overseen by committee of three, Bailey & Evans 511, Moses I-466;**39** trust closes, Moses I-466-467; **39** three-member penitentiary commission, Bailey & Evans 274; **40** ending despotic treatment of Southerners, Moses II-

810, Palmer 235; **40** civil service reform, Moses II-810; **40** tariff, Van Deusen 401; **40** attracts many members, Moses II-811, Palmer 235, 237; **40** Trumbull, Palmer 235, 237, Moses II-811; **40** Davis, Palmer 236, Moses II-811; **40-41** Rowett stumps for Palmer, Moses II-812; **41** Trumbull and Davis in running, Moses II-812, Palmer 240-241; **41** Rowett supports Greeley, *Chicago Tribune* July 14, 1887; **41** Palmer's career stalls, Palmer 243; **41** Trumbull suffers, Moses II-819; **41** ragged party lines and disposition to new parties, Palmer 244; **41** Reform Party described, Moses II-824, Palmer 244; **41** party beliefs, Moses II-825, *Illinois State Journal* June 11, 1874; **41** Rowett present, *Illinois State Journal* June 11, 1874, Moses II-824; **41** Palmer delivers address, *Illinois State Journal* June 11, 1874, Palmer 244-245, Moses II-825; **41** Rowett's resolution on standard of value, *Illinois State Journal* June 11, 1874, Moses II-825; **41-42** resolution to pay debts, *Illinois State Journal* June 11, 1874; **42** Rowett confronts Anderson, *Illinois State Journal* June 11, 1874; **42** submits nominations, Moses II-826, *Illinois State Journal* June 11, 1874; **42** did not attract voters, Moses II-825; **42** three seats available, *Carlinville Democrat* Nov. 23, 1876; **42** Wall, *History of Macoupin County 1879* 127, Moses II-1187, *Macoupin County Enquirer* Nov. 2, 1876; **42** English, *Macoupin County Enquirer* Nov. 2, 1876, Moses II-1170; **42** Powell, Moses II-1187, *Macoupin County Enquirer* Nov. 16, 1876, *Carlinville Democrat* Nov. 23, 1876; **42** Republicans elected governor, Howard 355; **42** control legislature, Moses II-1189; **42-43** Rowett "out in cold," *Macoupin County Enquirer* Oct. 5, 1876; **43** Rowett "blubbering," *Macoupin County Enquirer* Oct. 26, 1876; **43** Rowett in Montgomery County, *Macoupin County Enquirer* Oct. 12, 1876; **43** vote totals, *Macoupin County Enquirer* Nov. 16, 1876, *Carlinville Democrat* Nov. 23, 1876; **43** takes seat in January, Moses II-846; **43** leading member of legislature, *Illinois State Journal* July 14, 1887; **43** chair of committees, *Journal of Illinois H of R*; **43** issues Rowett supported, *Journal of Illinois H of R*; **43** votes for Logan, *Journal of Illinois H of R*; **43** active at 1880 convention, Moses II-862-863; **43** Grant and Blaine, Moses II-861-862, Neilson 57; **43** selection of delegates, Moses II-862-863, Neilson 57, Raum, 158-159; **44** Rowett for change, Moses II-862; **44** effects of change, Neilson 57; **44** Grant men win, Moses II-863, Raum 159, Neilson 57; **44** Rowett named delegate, Moses II-863, Raum 161; **44** seat contested, Raum 159-164, Moses II-865-866; **44** Rowett has last word, Neilson 57; **44** delegates admitted, Moses II-866, Raum 171; **44** anywhere from 302 to 309, Hesseltine 439, Smith 979; **44** remembered as "306," *Chicago Inter-Ocean* July 14, 1887, Smith 985; **44** nomination to Garfield, Smith 982-985, Moses II-866, Hesseltine 439; **44** Rowett corresponds with R.T. Lincoln, Rowett letters, **44** friends with Ingersoll, *Oregon Journal* July 15, 1932; **44** Ingersoll description, Malone IX-469-470; **44** friends with Raum, *Chicago Tribune* July 14, 1887; **44** Raum sketch, Boatner 681, Moses II-1201; **44-45** presides over 1880 convention, Moses II-862, Raum 158; **45** candidate in 1883, Moses II-880, Howard 167, Neilson 65-66; **45** Rowett campaigns for Raum, *Chicago Tribune* July 14, 1887; **45** Cullom speaks highly, *Chicago Inter-Ocean* July 14, 1887; **45** Raum again candidate, Moses II-917; **45** Rowett works for Farwell, *Chicago Tribune* July 14, 1887, *Chicago Inter-Ocean* July 14, 1887; **45** Farwell background, Moses II-917-918, Neilson 55; **45** close ally of Logan, *Chicago Tribune* July 14, 1887, *Chicago Inter-Ocean* July 14, 1887, *New York Times* July 14, 1887; **45** Logan, Boatner 486-487, Moses II-799-800, Palmer 257-258; **45** Rowett appointed through Logan's favor, *Chicago Tribune* July 14, 1887; **45** Arthur appoints, *New York Times* July 14, 1887, *Illinois State Journal* July 14, 1887, *Chicago Inter-Ocean* July 14, 1887; **45** Raum as commissioner, Raum 323; **45** lives at Tremont House, *Quincy City Directory 1882-83*; **45** Locust and 24th, *Quincy City Directory 1884-85*; **45** Joe gets work, *Quincy City Directory 1884-85*, Rowett letters; **45** Babcock angered, Rowett letters; **46** holds office until 1885, *Chicago Tribune* July 14, 1887, *Illinois State Journal* July 14, 1887, *New York Times* July 14, 1887; **46** Rowett speaks against divisions, *Chicago Tribune* July 14, 1887; **46** note, "Rowett never lost opportunity...," *Chicago Tribune* July 14, 1887.

Surprisingly little has been written on Rowett since his death, and what has been published has sometimes been inaccurate. The most obvious inaccuracy is the claim that Rowett raised Spokane, and that is disputed in such credible sources as Nardinger's exhaustive study of Spokane as well as Scott and Leach. Many other sources also tell the true story of Spokane's breeding and birth.

Nardinger's fascinating work is the leading historical source on Spokane's racing career. Rowett's place in racing is also documented in such period reference works as the *American Stud Books* and the *Nominations to Stakes and Declarations*. Tansey describes The Meadows in her recollections, while bits and pieces of information on the farm and Rowett's stature in the turf may be found in Carlinville and Chicago newspapers over a span of many years.

47 Richard and Joseph save money, Tansey 37; **47** substantial pay, Tansey 37, Boatner 624; **47** acquire and replace ordinary mares, Tansey 37; **47** Charley takes up residence, Tansey 37, *Carlinville Democrat* Nov. 23, 1865; **47** western and southern tracks, *Chicago Inter-Ocean* July 14, 1887; **47** races in Chicago, *Chicago Inter-Ocean* July 14, 1887, *Krik's Guide* 128; **47** Rowett colors, *Nominations to Stakes 1885-86*; **47** unique fashion of names, Fitzgerald letter; **47** performances long remembered, *Chicago Inter-Ocean* July 14, 1887; **47** away from home, *Illinois State Register* July 16, 1887; **47** Saratoga and Kentucky, *Chicago Tribune* July 14, 1887; **48** descriptions of Rowett's honesty, *Chicago Inter-Ocean* July 14, 1887; **48** size of farm, *Portrait and Biographical Record* 206, Macoupin County grantee/grantor records, probate records; **48** box stalls, *Macoupin County Enquirer* Apr. 11, 1940; **48** cost of barn, *Macoupin County Enquirer* Apr. 11, 1940; **49** barn thought to be largest in county, *Carlinville Democrat* Feb. 25, 1929; **49** leases additional tract, *Carlinville Democrat* July 3, 1929, *Macoupin County Enquirer* Apr. 11, 1940; **49** Rowett likes farming, *Chicago*

102

Chicago Inter-Ocean July 14, 1887.

Chapter IX -- Beagles

Rowett's name appears in just about every source on beagling that the researcher may want to use. Leading sources such as Lentilhon, Hochwalt, Columbo, Whitney, and Musladin offer much insight, but they are by no means the only volumes that refer to Rowett or that contribute to the history of beagling. As with Musladin, many newer works provide more concise information on beagling, but older publications should never be overlooked.

52 imports from English packs, Musladin 5; **52** recognized as best, Columbo 27, Hochwalt 18; **52** dates of first importation--1850s Arnn 17; 1860, Vriends-Parent 69; early 1870s, Hochwalt 18, Columbo 27; 1875, Lentilhon 178; 1876, Musladin 5; late 1870s, Prentice 33; early 1800s, Clark 14; **52-53** recollections by Joe's wife, Tansey 34-45; **53** small hounds called beagles, Columbo 27, Whitney 20, Hochwalt 18; **53** "so-called beagles," Hochwalt 18; **53** scarcely resembled today's beagles, Columbo 27, Whitney 20, Clark 14; **53** only slight resemblance to dachshunds and bassets, Columbo 27; **53** mostly white coat, Whitney 20, Clark 14; **53** Rowett introduces true-bred beagle, Hochwalt 18, Clark 14, Columbo 27; **53** Dolly shipped by brother-in-law, Rowett letters; **53** Rosey and Sam, Hochwalt 18, Columbo 28; **53** north of England, *Macoupin County Enquirer* Mar. 28, 1940; **53** size, color, conformity seen in today's dogs, Columbo 27, Clark 14, Hochwalt 18; **53** last word in breeding, Hochwalt 18; **53** unequalled bench show form, Hochwalt 18; **53** field ability, Hochwalt 18; **53** proud to find Rowetts in pedigree, Columbo 28; **53** strain scattered, Hochwalt 18; **53** Rowett dogs as recognized ones, Hochwalt 18; **53** need for standard arises, Lentilhon 52, Hochwalt 19; **53** formation of American-English Beagle Club, Musladin 5, Hochwalt 19; **53** founded by Philadelphia-area breeders, Musladin 5; **53** committee to draft standard, Hochwalt 19, Lentilhon 42, 51-52, Prentice 40; **54**

standard molded on Rowett beagles, Lentilhon 15, 173, 210, Whitney 20; **54** finest of time, Lentilhon 173, 178, Whitney 20, Hochwalt 18; **54** Rowett writes little of standard, Lentilhon 52; **54** Twadell's story, Lentilhon 52; **54** becomes first AKC standard, Musladin 5; **54** Rowett turns down presidency, Rowett letters; **54** expresses interest in lesser position, Rowett letters; **54** NBC founded in 1887, Jones & Hamilton 321; **54** ABC refuses to sanction, Musladin 5, Prentice 42; **54** clubs merge, Prentice 42-43; **54** standard revised, Musladin 5; **54** document remains much the same, Prentice 21-24, Arnn 22; **54** stock taken over after death, Hochwalt 21, Whitney 21, Prentice 35-36; **54** renowned descendants, Hochwalt 21; **54-55** Rowett strain remains best, Hochwalt 21, Prentice 33, Lentilhon 178-179; **55** few realize importance, *Macoupin County Enquirer* Apr. 11, 1940; **55** sales appear in estate, probate records; **55** note, Hochwalt 19, Prentice 33.

Chapter X -- Private Life

The 1891 *Portrait and Biographical Record of Macoupin County* provides some insight into the private life of the General. Information on the births of the children is found in the Macoupin County birth records, the family Bible, and the obituaries of the children. The successful traits of the children are also described in their obituaries as well as in the Tansey recollections.

56 re-marries, marriage records, *Macoupin County Enquirer* Sept. 2, 1914, *Portrait and Biographical Record* 206; **56** Ella, *Macoupin County Enquirer* Sept. 2, 1914; **56** Ellison, *Portrait and Biographical Record* 306; **56** Ella's spirit, *Macoupin County Enquirer* Sept. 2, 1914; **56** Mary, Rowett family Bible, *Carlinville Democrat* Sept. 27, 1923; **56** son born 7-14-1887, birth records; **56** Edith, Rowett family Bible, birth records; **56** Richard, *Carlinville Democrat* Feb. 28, 1929, Rowett family Bible; **56** Archibel, Rowett family Bible; **56** beagles not special, *Macoupin County Enquirer* Apr. 11, 1940; **56** children visit Rowett home, *Carlinville Democrat*

Feb. 28, 1929; **57** exercising the beagles, *Macoupin County Enquirer* Apr. 11, 1940; **57** described as handsome, Austin 10, *Quincy Daily Journal* July 14, 1887, *Chicago Inter-Ocean* July 14, 1887; **57** member of G.A.R., *Carlinville Democrat* July 21, 1887, *Chicago Inter-Ocean* July 14, 1887; **57** attended Presbyterian Church with no denomination, *Chicago Inter-Ocean* July 14, 1887; **57** Rowett away from home, *Illinois State Register* July 16, 1887; **57** devotion to home, *Illinois State Register* July 16, 1887.

Chapter XI -- The Legend of Bay Charley

Virtually all information for this chapter came from the July 3, 1929 edition of the *Carlinville Democrat*. That issue contained an article that quotes a letter from Edith Rowett Reeves telling of how the poem came to be. The poem is reprinted in its entirety in the paper. Ambrose also makes several references to Charley, some of which are cited in earlier chapters.

Chapter XII -- "Died in His Stable"

The various obituaries of Rowett's death provide some of the most thorough, consise biographies ever written on the General. Some, like the *Chicago Tribune*, give a detailed record of Rowett's last days.

The *Chicago Inter-Ocean* also provides excellent detail both of Rowett's life and his death. Both Springfield papers covered Rowett's death, albeit in differing fashion, as did the Carlinville papers, which mainly reprinted articles from either the Springfield or Chicago dailies. The *New York Times*, as well as the *Quincy Daily Journal*, also made front-page news of Rowett's death.

Descriptions of other events of Rowett's later life come from the Carlinville papers or from unpublished research.

63 left for Lexington, *Chicago Tribune* July 14, 1887; **63** sorrowful telegram, *Chicago Tribune* July 14, 1887; **63** Archibel's date of death and description, Rowett family Bible; **63** Rowett's health declines, *Chicago Tribune* July 14, 1887; **63** "either from shock or progression...," *Chicago Tribune* July 14, 1887; **63** suffered several spells, *Chicago Inter-Ocean* July 14, 1887; **63** diagnosed with rheumatism, *Chicago Tribune* July 14, 1887; **63** "unable to go any distance...," *Chicago Tribune* July 14, 1887; **63** keynote speaker, *Carlinville Democrat* May 12, 1887; **65** tornado episode, Stoddard 3; **65** meets reporter and tries to cross track, *Chicago Tribune* July 14, 1887; **65** up and down stairs, *Chicago Tribune* July 14, 1887; **65** episode with field glasses, *Chicago Tribune* July 14, 1887; **65** "Rowett acknowledged...," *Chicago Tribune* July 14, 1887; **65** colts arrive, *Chicago Tribune* July 14, 1887; **65** complains to two men, *Chicago Tribune* July 14, 1887; **66** memorial presentation, *Chicago Tribune* July 12, 1887; **66** friend Strattan, *Illinois State Journal* July 14, 1887; **66** Strattan's background, Moses II-875, 1185; **66** Rowett in excellent health, *Illinois State Journal* July 14, 1887; **66** Strattan rides with Rowett, *Illinois State Journal* July 14, 1887; **66** find colt dead, *Chicago Tribune* July 14, 1887; **66** walked across field, *Chicago Tribune* July 14, 1887; **66** bill of $24, *Chicago Tribune* July 14, 1887, *Chicago Inter-Ocean* July 14, 1887; **66** boy swore bill paid, *Chicago Tribune* July 14, 1887; **66** Rowett demands bill, *Chicago Inter-Ocean* July 14, 1887; **66** believed being taken, *Chicago Inter-Ocean* July 14, 1887; **66** raises arm, *Chicago Tribune* July 14, 1887; **66** calls out, *Chicago Tribune* July 14, 1887, *Chicago Inter-Ocean* July 14, 1887; **66** falls heavily against stall, *Chicago Tribune* July 14, 1887; **66** face dark purple, *Chicago Inter-Ocean* July 14, 1887; **66** carried out and rubbed with camphor, *Chicago Tribune* July 14, 1887; **66** one or two gasps, *Chicago Tribune* July 14, 1887; **67** physicians arrive, *Quincy Daily Journal* July 14, 1887; **67** Joe arrives, *Chicago Inter-Ocean* July 14, 1887; **67** effects of wounds responsible; *Illinois State Register* July 16, 1887; **67** Joe sends telegram to Ella, *Carlinville Democrat* July 14, 1887; **67** Ella stricken down, *Illinois State Journal* July 14, 1887;

67 others learn of news, sources given; **67** Palmer receives dispatch and leaves, *Illinois State* Journal July 14, 1887; **67** special train, *Illinois State Journal* July 14, 1887; **67** Carlinville in mourning, *Illinois State Register* July 16, 1887; **67** highest number of mourners, *Carlinville Democrat* July 21, 1887; **67** ceremonial escort, *Carlinville Democrat* July 21, 1887; **67** military record read, *Illinois State Register* July 16, 1887, *Carlinville Democrat* July 21, 1887; **67** Palmer overcome, *Illinois State Register* July 16, 1887, *Carlinville Democrat* July 21, 1887; **67** women pin flag, *Illinois State Register* July 16, 1887, *Carlinville Democrat* July 21, 1887; **67** viewed by long line of mourners, *Carlinville Democrat* July 21, 1887; **67** choir serenades, *Carlinville Democrat* July 21, 1887.

Chapter XIII -- Legacy

Details of Rowett's estate are found in the probate records of Macoupin County. The later years of Ella and the children are described in their obituaries as well as in Tansey's recollections. Of the four children who survived Rowett, information on Charles is by far the most difficult to find.

69 personal estate, probate records; **69** sales of stock, probate records; **69** claims and double mortgage, probate records; **69** money left to be divided, probate records; **69** Joe works for petroleum compnay, probate records, *Chicago Inter-Ocean* July 14, 1887; **69** lands position at Joliet, *Macoupin County Argus* June 25, 1903, *Macoupin Daily Enquirer* June 23, 1903; **69** marries Charlotte Chapman, Tansey 37, *Macoupin County Argus* June 25, 1903, marriage records; **69** works with World's Fair, *Macoupin County Argus* June 25, 1903; **69** returns to penitentiary, *Macoupin Daily Enquirer* June 23, 1903, *Carlinville Democrat* June 25, 1903; **69** health declines, U.S. Military Pension Records--J. Rowett; **70** Joe dies, *Macoupin County Argus* June 25, 1903, *Macoupin Daily Enquirer* June 23, 1903; **70** Charles graduates, Stoddard 3; **70**

Charles marries, moves, Tansey 38; **70** Colorado, probate records; **70** lower California, Tansey 38; **70** Charles' children, Tansey 38-39; **70** Mary and Edith graduate from Blackburn, Stoddard 3; **70** Mary is postmistress, *Carlinville Democrat* Sept. 27, 1923; **70** Mary attractive and intelligent, Tansey 39-40; **70** Mary marries, *Carlinville Democrat* Sept. 27, 1923; **70** Edith follows to Chicago, Tansey 39; **70** Richard, Jr. stays, *Carlinville Democrat* Feb. 28, 1929; **70** family dream, Tansey 39; **70** Ella loves farm life and nature, *Macoupin County Enquirer* Sept. 2, 1914; **70** Richard builds ranch, Tansey 41; **70** Mary returns to Chicago, Tansey 40; **70** works for Wise and is editor, *Carlinville Democrat* Sept. 27, 1923, Tansey 40-41; **70** Mary dies, *Carlinville Democrat* Sept. 27, 1923; **70-71** Edith leaves Nebraska for Chicago, California, and Oregon, Tansey 41; **71** marries Reeves, Tansey 41, *1906 Seventh Reunion Proceedings* 36; **71** profitable idea, Tansey 41; **71** Edith dies, *Oregon Journal* June 28, 1951; **71** Ella, *Macoupin County Enquirer* Sept. 2, 1914; **71** laughs about birthday and anniversary, *Macoupin County Enquirer* Sept. 2, 1914; **71** Ella dies, *Macoupin County Enquirer* Sept. 2, 1914; **71** Richard, Jr., *Carlinville Democrat* Feb. 28, 1929; **71** Richard, Jr. dies, *Carlinville Democrat* Feb. 28, 1929; **71** Spokane's debut, Nardinger 39; **72** Cullom's words, *Chicago Inter-Ocean* July 14, 1887;

Note on the Author

Tom Emery, a longtime enthusiast and researcher of history, received his B.A. with degrees in business administration, accounting, and economics from Blackburn College in 1993 and his M.B.A. from Southern Illinois University at Edwardsville in 1995.

Although this is his first full-length book, Emery, a free-lance writer, has extensive experience in many disciplines of writing. Twenty-six years of age at the publishing of this book, Emery is single and lives in Carlinville.

Please send me _____ copies of *Richard Rowett: Thoroughbreds, Beagles, and the Civil War* at $12.95 each (Illinois residents add .81 sales tax) plus $2.00 shipping and handling for the first book—$1.00 for each additional book.

Name _____

Address _____

City_____ State_____ Zip _____

Please make check or money order payable to
History in Print and send to:
HISTORY IN PRINT
337 E. Second South St.
Carlinville, IL 62626

Please send me _____ copies of *Richard Rowett: Thoroughbreds, Beagles, and the Civil War* at $12.95 each (Illinois residents add .81 sales tax) plus $2.00 shipping and handling for the first book—$1.00 for each additional book.

Name _____

Address _____

City_____ State_____ Zip _____

Please make check or money order payable to
History in Print and send to:
HISTORY IN PRINT
337 E. Second South St.
Carlinville, IL 62626